INDIAN HISTORY

INDIAN HISTORY

ASIATIC AND EUROPEAN

JAMES TALBOYS WHEELER

GYAN

Published by

GYAN

Gyan Publishing House
5, Ansari Road
Daryaganj, New Delhi-110002
Phone: 011-47034999, 9811692060
E-mail: books@gyanbooks.com

Distribution Network
gyanbooks.com
India, USA, Canada, UK, Australia

ISBN: 978-93-7169-302-8 (PB)

First Published, 1906

2nd Impression 2025

Printed at: Gyan Press, Delhi.

INDIAN HISTORY

Author: JAMES TALBOYS WHEELER

INDIAN HISTORY

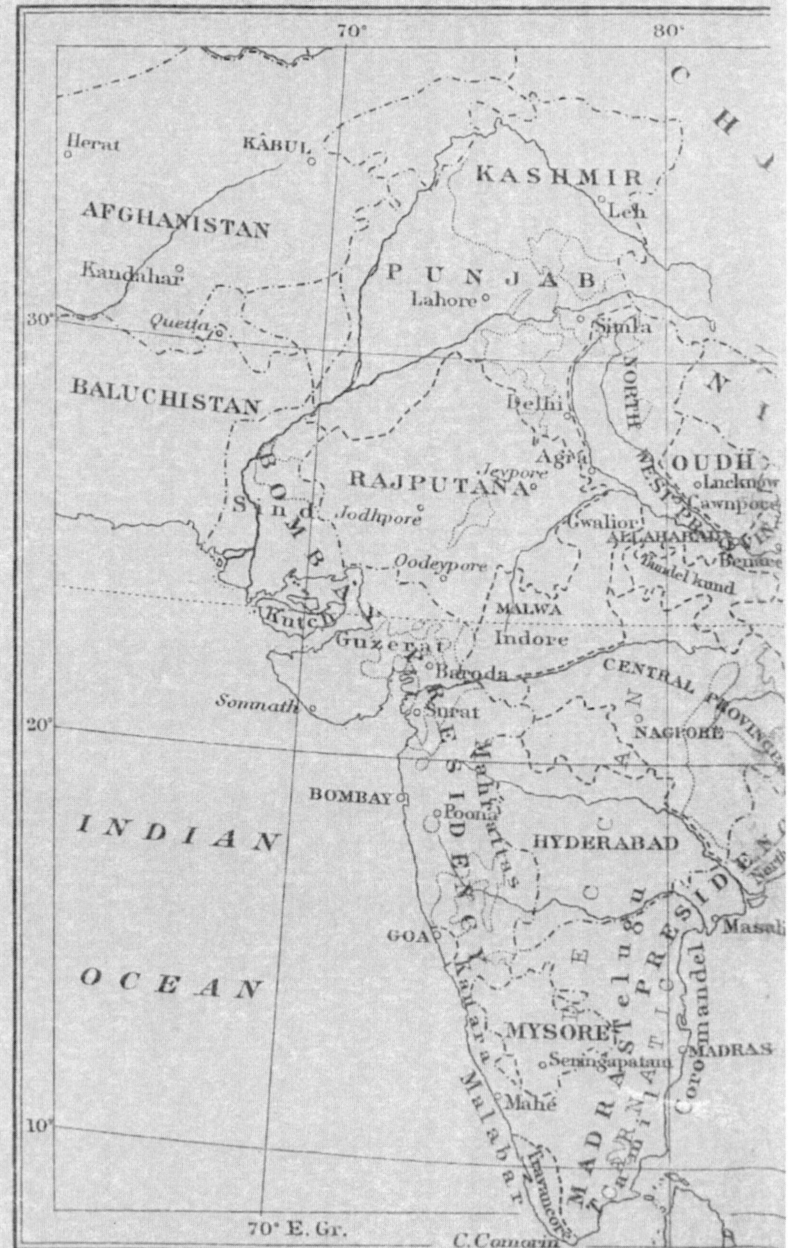
70°
80°
Herat
KÂBUL
KASHMIR
Leh
AFGHANISTAN
Kandahar
PUNJAB
Lahore
Quetta
Simla
BALUCHISTAN
Delhi
NORTH WEST
Agra
OUDH
Jeypore
RAJPUTANA
Sind
Jodhpore
Gwalior
ALLAHABAD
BOMBAY
Oodeypore
Bundel kund
MALWA
Kutch
Indore
Guzerat
Baroda
CENTRAL PROVINCES
Somnath
Surat
NAGPORE
Mahrattas
BOMBAY
Poona
HYDERABAD
INDIAN
PRESIDENCY
DECCAN
GOA
Telugu
OCEAN
Kanara
Coromandel
MYSORE
MADRAS
Seringapatam
Malabar
Mahé
CARNATIC
Travancore
70° E. Gr.
C. Comorin
30°
20°
10°

London: Macn

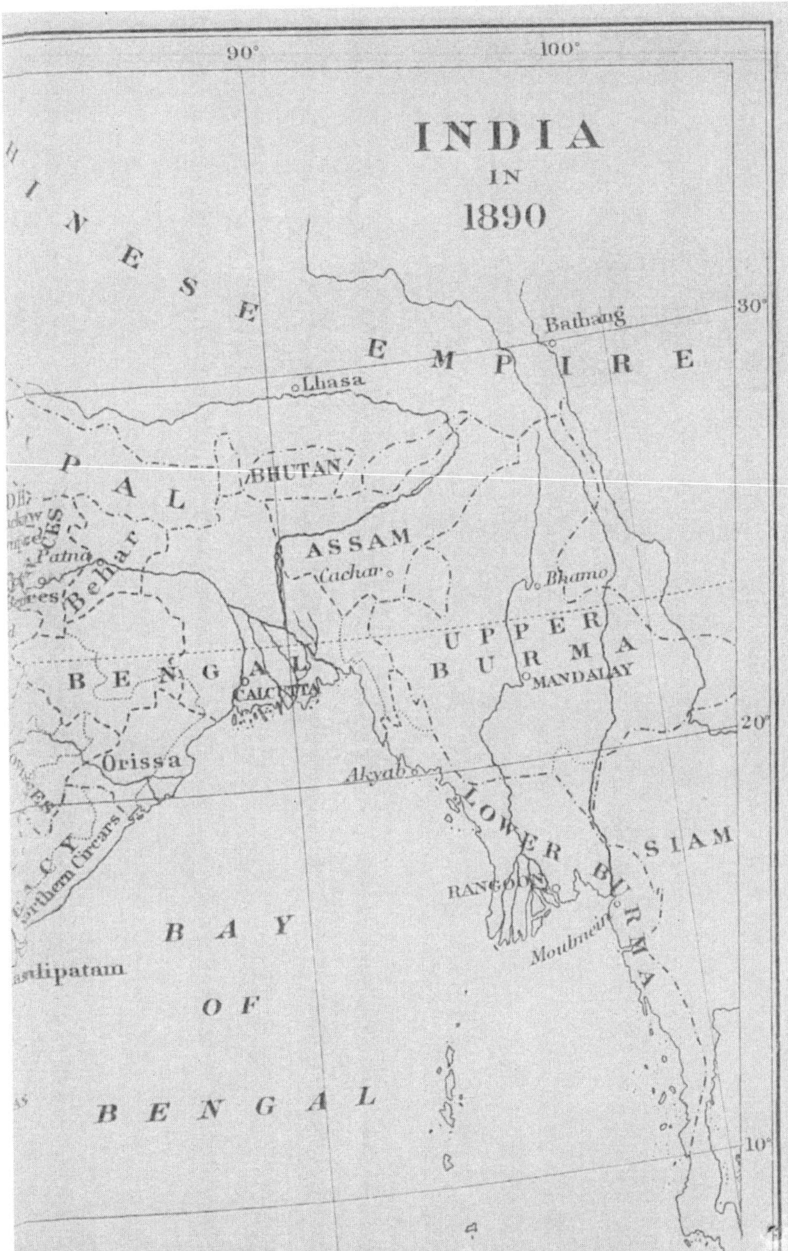

Stanford's Geogl. Estabt.

acmillan & Co.

INDIAN HISTORY

Asiatic and European

BY

J. TALBOYS WHEELER

Late Assistant-Secretary to the Government of India, Foreign Department, and late Secretary to the Government of British Burma. Author of "History of India from the Earliest Ages," including the "Maha Bharata" and "Ramayana," "A Short History of India," &c., &c.

1890

CONTENTS.

CHAPTER VIII.

CHAPTER IX.

CHAPTER X.

CHAPTER XI.

CHAPTER XII.

CHAPTER XIII.

PRIMER

OF

INDIAN HISTORY.

CHAPTER I.

HINDUS BEFORE THE MOHAMMEDAN CONQUEST, *ante* A.D. 1000.

1. Punjab, or "Land of Five Rivers": Origin of Caste.—2. Hindustan, or "Land of Hindus."—3. Hindus of Bengal, Deccan and Peninsula.—4. Vedic Aryans.—5. Non-Vedic People.—6. Rise of Buddhism.—7. Vishnu and Siva.—8. Rama and Krishna.—9. Rama of Ayodhya, or Oudh.—10. Wars against Ravana, King of the Demons.—11. Krishna of Mathura and Vrindavana.—12. War of the Mahabharata: Pandavas and Kauravas.—13. Pandava Settlement at Old Delhi.—14. Gambling Match: Pandavas lose Indra-prastha.—15. Eighteen Days' Battle at Kuru-kshetra, or Paniput.—16. Krishna and the Pandavas.—17. Persians, Greeks, and Scythians.—18. Summary.

1. **Punjab, or "Land of Five Rivers": Origin of Caste.**—History begins in India with the Aryan conquest of the Punjab. These Aryans were more or less related to Persia, and are called Vedic, because they worshipped the gods of the oldest Veda. They were a fair-complexioned people, who settled as colonists in the valleys of the Indus and its five tributaries, namely, the Jhelum, Chenab, Ravi, Beyas, and Sutlej. They belonged to three types or grades of men who eventually fossilized into castes, namely.

the priest, the warrior, and the merchant. In later history they appeared as the Brahman or sacred caste, the Kshatriya or royal caste, and the Vaisya or merchant caste. There was also a fourth caste, who cultivated the soil and were known as Sudras. In the present day the Brahmans follow almost any profession; the Kshatriyas have disappeared, or are only known as Rajputs; the Vaisyas have nearly merged into the Sudras; whilst the Sudras have become the great middle-class of India, and are split up into a number of hereditary sub-castes, according to their trade or occupation.

2. **Hindustan, or "Land of Hindus."**—The people of the Punjab were called Indians or Hindus, after the river Indus. They invaded the valleys of the Jumna and Ganges, which flow in a south-easterly direction towards the Bay of Bengal, but they were still called Hindus, and the region between the Punjab and Bengal was known as Hindustan, or the "Land of Hindus." Hindustan extends eastward to Bengal, and southward to the Deccan, and the conquering race claim to be Kshatriyas, and are called Rajputs, or "sons of Rajas."

3. **Hindus of Bengal, Deccan and Peninsula.**—Bengal and the Deccan were thus outlying regions, and the people belonged to different races and spoke different tongues. The bulk were brought under the caste system and were known as Hindus, although they might never have seen or heard of the river Indus. Thus people like the Bengalis of the east, the Mahrattas and Gonds of the Deccan, and the Telugu, Tamil, Kanarese and other Dravidian races of the remote south, or Peninsula, are all called to this day by the common name of Hindus.

4. **Vedic Aryans.**—The Vedic Aryans in the

Punjab and Hindustan worshipped the Sun and other powers of nature with hymns and sacrifices. The Brahmans worshipped Agni, or fire; the Kshatriyas worshipped Indra, the god of rain and thunder; and the Vaisyas worshipped Varuna, the god of the sea. Sometimes all these gods were worshipped, each in turn as the Supreme Being, as well as a host of other divinities of the earth, air, and sky. The peaceful castes offered the sacred homa, or rice, milk, butter, and curds. The Kshatriyas, as royal warriors, sacrificed horses, cattle, and other animals, to the gods, which were afterwards eaten by the priests and worshippers.

5. **Non-Vedic People.**—The non-Vedic people were to be found all over India, but especially in the regions outside the Punjab and Hindustan, such as Bengal, Deccan, and Peninsula. They worshipped divinities associated with the mysteries of birth, death, and the transmigrations of the soul after death; propitiating them with noisy music and orgiastic rites, whilst many votaries led the lives of naked mendicants, tortured themselves as a religious merit, and pondered over the bones and ashes of the dead.

6. **Rise of Buddhism.**—Gautama Buddha, who flourished in the fifth century before Christ, taught a new religion. He declared that neither sacrifices nor prayers, orgies nor austerities, would deliver the soul from the miseries of endless transmigrations; that purity in thought, word, and deed, lovingkindness towards the whole animal creation, obedience to parents and pastors, and abstinence from all intoxicating things, would alone avert evil and secure happiness either in this life or in lives to come; that those however who were truly wise and sought deliverance from the endless chain of transmigrations, would abstain from all gratifications that bound the

soul to the universe of being, until they had extinguished every affection, passion, and desire, and found eternal rest in nirvána.

7. **Vishnu and Siva.**—At a later period new teachers appeared and restored the worship of the gods, and taught that all the gods were merged into one divine spirit who might be worshipped as Vishnu or as Siva. That Vishnu, the divine Sun that illuminates the universe, would receive his worshippers after death in a heaven of bliss. That Siva, the divine spirit of goodness and purity, would absorb the souls of his worshippers in his own spiritual essence. Each god was married to a goddess who presided over mortals. Lakshmi, the goddess of prosperity, was the wife of Vishnu. Durga, the goddess of the household, was the wife of Siva.

8. **Rama and Krishna.**—Vishnu is the Sun. He is said to have become incarnate in ten avatars. Two of these avatars are associated with the past history of India, namely, Rama, the hero of Ayodhya or Oudh, and Krishna, the hero of Mathura or Muttra. The legends of Rama are told in the Sanskrit epic known as the Ramayana. The legends of Krishna are mixed up with the story of the great war between rival kinsmen of the house of Bharata, which is told in the Mahabharata.

9. **Rama of Ayodhya, or Oudh.**—Rama is the divine hero of Ayodhya, a kingdom which covered the greater part of Hindustan. The Rajputs, who call themselves children of the Sun, claim Rama as their divine ancestor. He was born as the eldest son of a Maharaja of Ayodhya by the first wife, but was banished by his father from the court and kingdom in order to secure the throne for a younger son by the third wife. Rama, in obedience to his father's

commands, went away with his wife Sita and his brother Lakshmana into the southern jungles; and Sita was carried off by Rávana, the king of the demons, or Rákshasas, and shut up in an impregnable fortress in the island of Lanka, or Ceylon.

10. **Wars against Rávana, King of the Demons.**—Rama formed an alliance with Hanuman, the king of the monkeys, who commanded an army of monkeys in the war against Rávana. These monkeys are said to have been gods born on earth in monkey forms to help Rama. According to the Rámáyana, they built a bridge, or rather a causeway, over the straits between India and Ceylon, by bringing huge rocks and boulders from the Himálaya mountains. Rávana was slain; Sita was delivered from her captivity and brought back to Ayodhya, where Rama was restored to his throne and kingdom.

11. **Krishna of Mathura and Vrindavana.**—Krishna is the hero of the Yadavas, a wandering tribe of cowherds. His early life was divided between Mathura and Vrindavana on the river Jumna, and the rural encampment at Gokula on the opposite bank. He is said to have been of royal descent, but was brought up in the family of a cowherd at Gokula. His early exploits are popular with the Hindus. He upset churns and shared the butter with his playfellows. He played on the flute and danced with the milkmaids. He fought against the Raja of Mathura, and took possession of the throne and kingdom. He married many princesses and was famous for love adventures. Eventually his kingdom was invaded by an army of Indo-Scythians, and he migrated with all his wives and people to the city of Dwaraka in Guzerat, and dwelt there many years.

12. **War of the Mahabharata: Pandavas**

and Kauravas.—This famous war was fought in a land partly Punjab and partly Hindustan. The city of Hastinapur, on the upper Ganges, was the capital of the great kingdom of Bharata. Pandu, the Maharaja, had five sons called the Pandavas, of whom Yudhishthira was the eldest. Pandu abdicated the throne and retired into the jungles. His brother, a blind prince, reigned in his room at Hastinapur. He had several sons, known as the Kauravas, of whom Duryodhana was the eldest. Consequently there was rivalry between the two families; and the question was whether Yudhishthira the Pandava, or Duryodhana the Kaurava, should succeed to the throne of Hastinapur on the death of the blind Maharaja.

13. **Pandava Settlement at Old Delhi.**—Yudhishthira was appointed "Little Raja," and would have succeeded to the kingdom of Hastinapur on the death of his blind uncle, the Maharaja, or "Great Raja;" but Duryodhana and the Kauravas clamoured against their father for promoting his nephews instead of his sons. The Pandavas were sent into exile, and Duryodhana was appointed "Little Raja." During the exile Yudhishthira married Draupadi, the daughter of the Maharaja of Panchala (? Punjab). The Kauravas were alarmed at the alliance, and consented to a division of the kingdom; Hastinapur remaining with Duryodhana and the Kauravas, whilst the southern jungles round the spot where Delhi now stands were made over to Yudhishthira and the Pandavas.

14. **Gambling Match: Pandavas lose Indraprastha.**—The Pandavas cleared the jungles, and founded the city and fort of Indra-prastha, and the ruins at Old Delhi on the upper Jumna may be seen to this day. The Kauravas envied their good fortune. They invited the Pandavas to a gambling match at

Hastinapur, cheated them out of their wealth and kingdom, and insulted Draupadi, the wife of Yudhishthira, by calling her a slave girl. The blind Maharaja interfered to prevent a deadly feud. Yudhishthira and his brethren were sent into exile for thirteen years, and Duryodhana and his brethren remained in possession of the two kingdoms.

15. **Eighteen Days' Battle at Kuru-kshetra, or Paniput.**—When the exile was over the Pandavas demanded the restoration of Indra-prastha, but the Kauravas refused, and both sides prepared for war. The great battle was fought on the plain of Kuru-kshetra, the modern Paniput. It lasted eighteen days. It consisted mostly of single combats interspersed with supernatural exploits. It ended in the slaughter of the Kauravas, the burning of the dead, the lamentations of widows and daughters, and the installation of Yudhishthira on the throne of the united kingdoms of Hastinapur and Indra-prastha.

16. **Krishna and the Pandavas.**—Krishna is represented throughout the Mahabharata as the divine protector of the Pandavas. He rescued Draupadi, the wife of Yudhishthira, from the insults of the Kauravas after the gambling match. He went to Hastinapur to persuade the Kauravas to restore Indra-prastha to the Pandavas. He is said to have revealed himself to the Kauravas as the Supreme Being, in all the brightness of the sun, with flames of fire issuing from his eyes and ears. When the war was over he was the consoler of the blind Maharaja and his wife for the loss of their sons the Kauravas. Eventually he returned to Dwaraka, where his kinsmen slaughtered one another at a banquet; the city was destroyed by a cyclone, and he himself was slain by the random shot of a hunter.

17. **Persians, Greeks, and Scythians.**—The Punjab was a satrapy of the old Persian empire in the days of Darius and Xerxes in the sixth and fifth centuries before Christ. It was invaded by the Greeks under Alexander the Great in the fourth century before Christ. It was a battle-ground between Græco-Bactrians of Central Asia and Rajput kings of Hindustan, as well as between Indo-Scythians and Rajputs, during centuries of unrecorded history. Finally it was conquered by the Mohammedans in the eleventh and twelfth centuries of the Christian era.

18. **Summary.**—India is thus a continent in itself, cut off from the rest of Asia by the Himálaya, or "abode of snow." The people are known as Hindus, and this name is applied to Aryans and non-Aryans, and indeed to all, whatever may be the differences of race or language, who are divided into castes and worship the gods of the Brahmans. But outside these masses of Hindus are barbarian peoples who inhabit the hills and jungles. They are sometimes called "aborigines," but are better known as "non-Hindus," as they are not divided into castes, and have gods and priests of their own. These non-Hindus are gradually being brought under the Brahmanical system. They are divided into castes by Brahmanical influence. Their gods are accepted by their new teachers, but represented as forms, types or avatars of one or other great gods, Vishnu or Siva, or of their respective goddesses Lakshmi or Durga. This conversion from barbarism to Brahmanism, or, as it may be called, this transformation of non-Hindus into Hindus, has been probably going on from time immemorial.

CHAPTER II.

MOHAMMEDAN EMPIRE, A.D. 570-1525.

1. Arabia and India.—2. Arab Merchants and Carriers.—3 Mohammed and his Koran, A.D. 570–632.—4. Arab Caliphs at Medina, Damascus, and Bagdad: Conquest of Sind.—5. Revolt of Turks against the Arabs.—6. Mahmud of Ghazni, 997-1030: Turkish Invasions of the Punjab and Hindustan.—7. Mahmud's War against Somnath: Destruction of his Army.—8. Afghan Uprising: Conquest of Punjab, Hindustan, and Bengal, 1180–1290.—9. Rajput Migrations to the South.—10. Conquest of Deccan and Peninsula, 1290–1316.—11. Hindu Revolt at Delhi: New Capital at Tughlakabad, 1320.—12. Tughlak Sultans, 1320–1398.—13. "Timur the Tartar" invades Northern India, 1398–99.—14. Anarchy: the Sayyids, 1399–1451.—15. Afghan Conquest: Lodi Dynasty, 1451–1526.—16. Summary.

1. **Arabia and India.**—Arabia is a peninsula nearly as vast as India, but it has no great rivers and very few towns or large villages. It is mostly desert, with oases of cultivation round springs and wells. The bulk of the Arabs are nomads, dwelling in tents and wandering about with goats and camels from pasture to pasture. Some however dwell at the ports on the sea coast, and become rich by trade.

2. **Arab Merchants and Carriers.**—In ancient times the Arabs crossed the Indian Ocean in boats, and bought cotton goods, spices, perfumes, precious stones, and other Indian products from the Hindus on the coast of Malabar. They carried their cargoes to Muscat, Aden and Mocha, and sent them through

the desert on the backs of camels to Egypt, Syria and Babylon. The Roman merchants cut off the land route by sending great ships down the Red Sea to India. The Arab tribes lost the carrying trade and their camels perished by thousands. They sank into poverty and barbarism. They went every year to Mecca to worship the idols in the Kaaba temple; but they were steeped in ignorance and superstition, putting their infant daughters to death, and practising other abominations.

3. **Mohammed and his Koran,** A.D. **570-632.** —Mohammed was born at Mecca in A.D. 570. When a young man he went on a trading journey to Syria, and saw something of Jews and Christians. At the age of forty he began to preach, declaring that he was a prophet sent by God to root out idolatry and restore the religion of Abraham. He set forth his religion in poems divided into **suras, or chapters,** which were known as the Koran. For many years he was persecuted by the Arabs at Mecca, but in A.D. 622 he fled to Medina, and his "hijra," or "flight," is the era of Islam to this day. At Medina he became known as the prophet of Arabia, waged war against all who refused to believe in his mission, destroyed the idols in the Kaaba at Mecca, and established Islam as the dominant faith. He promised a paradise of delights for all believers and a hell of torment for all unbelievers. He ordered his followers to abstain from wine and strong drink. He permitted them to marry as many wives as they pleased, not exceeding four, but all marriages of Mohammedans with unbelievers were strictly forbidden.

4. **Arab Caliphs at Medina, Damascus, and Bagdad: Conquest of Sind.**—Mohammed died A.D. 632. His successors were called caliphs. They were reverenced as popes in religious matters, and

obeyed as emperors in things temporal. They conquered Northern Africa and Spain on the western side, and Syria, Persia, and Central Asia on the eastern side. Four caliphs reigned in succession at Medina from 632 to 660. A second dynasty, known as Omeyads, reigned at Damascus from 660 to 750. About 712—714 the Arab armies advanced to the lower Indus, conquered the Rajputs of Sind, and compelled them to pay tribute. In 750 a third dynasty, known as Abassides, overthrew the Omeyad caliphs of Damascus, and began to reign at Bagdad. The Arab empire split in two. An Omeyad caliph reigned in Spain over a Western empire, whilst the Abassides reigned at Bagdad over an Eastern empire.

5. **Revolt of Turks against the Arabs.**—During the tenth century the Turks were rising against the Arabs. They were of Tartar origin, but had become Mohammedans. They were strong and brave, and many were engaged as bodyguards of the caliphs until they grew powerful and overruled their masters. Some founded kingdoms in Central Asia, such as Bokhara and Kabul, and reigned as independent Sultans; or advanced towards Western Asia, conquered Persia, Armenia, Syria, and Asia Minor, and founded empires under the names of Seljuk and Ottoman. In a word, they broke up the Arab supremacy, but reverenced the caliphs as the popes or pontiffs of Islam.

6. **Mahmud of Ghazni, 997-1030: Turkish Invasions of the Punjab and Hindustan.**—Mahmud of Ghazni was a famous Sultan of this type. He founded an empire which extended over Bokhara, Kábul (or Caubool), and Persia. He made twelve expeditions into the Punjab and Hindustan, which some have reckoned as sixteen. He was zealous for Islam, and for a long time was a bitter persecutor of the

Hindu religion. He broke down temples, destroyed idols, and carried away treasures of gold and jewels to his city of Ghazni. He also carried away so many thousands of Hindus into captivity that a slave could be bought for two rupees in the bazaars of Central Asia. But he could not force the Hindus to become Mohammedans. He annexed the Punjab to his dominions, and compelled the Rajput princes of Hindustan to pay tribute.

7. **Mahmud's War against Somnath: destruction of his Army.**—The last exploit of Mahmud was the most famous of all. His wrath had been kindled against the Brahmans of Somnath, who worshipped the god Siva in the island off the southern coast of Guzerat. The Brahmans boasted that Mahmud had destroyed the temples of Vishnu, but dared not touch the temples of Siva. Mahmud swore that he would destroy Somnath. It was a thousand miles from Ghazni, and the way lay through the burning desert of Sind. Mahmud reached Somnath in safety, and fulfilled his vow. He clove the pillar, which was sacred to Siva, with his battle-axe, and a heap of gold and jewels were scattered on the floor. He stayed a year in Guzerat and then went back to Ghazni. His army however was lost in the desert of Sind, and nearly all died of heat and thirst, or went mad in the burning sun. Mahmud escaped to Ghazni with a remnant of his army, but thousands of his soldiers perished in the sands.

8. **Afghan Uprising: Conquest of Punjab, Hindustan, and Bengal, 1180-1290.**—In the twelfth century the Turks of Ghazni succumbed to the Afghans of Ghor. The Afghans are Mohammedans with Jewish features. They are said to be descended from the ten tribes of Israel who were carried away captive by the King of Assyria, but the

tradition is obscure. Nothing for certain is known of them before the twelfth century, when they came down from the mountains of Ghor between Ghazni and Herat, captured Ghazni, and overturned the dynasty of Mahmud. Eventually they turned their backs on Ghazni, and conquered the Punjab, Hindustan, and Bengal. Henceforth they reigned at Delhi, where the Sultan Kutub-ud-din, the "pole star of the faith," built the Kutub, or "pole-star" tower to commemorate his victories.

9. **Rajput Migrations to the South.**—The Rajput princes were thus driven from their thrones in the valleys of the Ganges and Jumna, and went away with their kinsfolk and vassals to the south, where they founded new kingdoms in Rajputana between the Jumna and Nerbudda rivers. Here they reigned as Rajas, and the Rana of Chitor was their suzerain or "overlord."

10. **Conquest of Deccan and Peninsula, 1290-1316.**—Towards the end of the thirteenth century a Sultan reigned at Delhi who was bent on subduing all India. He was called Ala-ud-din, or the "glory of the faith." He conquered the Mahratta country in the Western Deccan, and compelled the Mahratta Raja to pay tribute. He conquered a Rajput kingdom in Guzerat, to the northward of the Mahratta country, and carried away the wife of the Rajput Raja, and made her his queen. He then invaded Rajputana, captured the strong fortress of Chitor, and carried off the Rana of Chitor, who was suzerain of all the Rajput princes. He wanted to marry the daughter of the Rana, but she escaped with her father from Delhi to Chitor. Last of all he sent an army to the Peninsula to invade the Telugu and Tamil kingdoms in the eastern plain, and the Kanaeres kingdom of Mysore, on the western table land. The

Mohammedan army plundered the Hindu temples and royal treasures, and brought away gold and jewels to the value of a hundred millions sterling. Ala-ud-din is the first Mohammedan Sultan who tried to subdue all India, or who married a Hindu princess. His name, pronounced Alá-úd-dín, is the same as the Aladdin of the *Arabian Nights*. He died in 1316.

11. **Hindu Revolt at Delhi: New Capital at Tughlakabad, 1320.**—After the death of Ala-ud-din there was a Hindu revolt at Delhi. Many excesses were committed by Hindu rebels within the city. The revolt spread to the Deccan and Peninsula. The Rajas who had been compelled to pay tribute by the general of Ala-ud-din, threw off the Mohammedan yoke. The Turkish Viceroy of the Punjab marched an army to Delhi, took the city by storm, and ascended the throne as the first Sultan of the house of Tughlak. He would not live at Delhi, but removed the capital to the strong fortress of Tughlakabad, or the "city of Tughlak," a few miles off.

12. **Tughlak Sultans, 1320-1398.**—The Tughlak Sultans were Turks. The founder of the dynasty was called Ghias-ud-din, or "champion of the faith." He died in 1325. His son and successor was named Mohammed Tughlak. He reconquered the Hindu Rajas in the south. He removed the people of Delhi to Deoghur in the Deccan, possibly to overawe the Rajas. But Deoghur was 800 miles from Delhi, and the people suffered so much by the removal that the Sultan ordered them to go back again. Mohammed Tughlak coined copper counters, and commanded his subjects to take them instead of money, without keeping any balance in gold or silver bullion. Meanwhile the people coined heaps of similar counters in their own houses, and paid the taxes with them. At last no one would take the counters, and the foreign merchants

would not sell their goods for anything but gold. There was no gold remaining in India. The treasury at Tughlakabad was crammed with copper, but no one would take it. The troops were without pay and the State was bankrupt. The Mohammedan army in the Deccan revolted and set up a Sultan of their own. Other revolts followed in Bengal, Guzerat, and elsewhere. Mohammed Tughlak died in 1350. His successor, Firuz Tughlak, inherited nothing but the Punjab and Hindustan. The new Sultan is praised by Mohammedan historians, but he destroyed Hindu temples and persecuted the Brahmans. He died in 1388, and India drifted into anarchy. The Mohammedans fought against each other, and the Hindus revolted against their supremacy.

13. **"Timur the Tartar" invades Northern India, 1398-99.**—Meanwhile "Timur the Tartar" was desolating half Asia. He had founded a kingdom in Bokhara and Kabul, and fixed his capital at Samarkand. He led his Tartar host westward through Persia, and then moved towards the north and invaded Russia to the neighbourhood of Moscow. In 1398-99 he marched through the Punjab to the city of Delhi, and was proclaimed Emperor of India. Such was the terror of his name that all the Sultans in India seem to have sent him presents by way of homage, and acknowledged themselves to be his vassals. He however would not stay in India. He carried away the treasures of Hindustan to his city of Samarkand, and then prepared to conquer Western Asia. Every Turk and Tartar prince in those days was anxious to reach Constantinople, which was still known as Roum or Rome; and Timur waged war against the Ottoman Bajazet, who was almost within grasp of the coveted city.

14. **Anarchy: the Sayyids, 1399-1451.**—After

Timur left India Delhi fell into anarchy. Later on a Sayyid, or holy man said to be descended from the Prophet, restored order in the city and environs, and was succeeded in turn by three others of like character. The dynasty is known as that of the Sayyids or Syuds. But Delhi was no longer the metropolis of an empire, and for many years very little is known of Northern India that can be called history.

15. **Afghan Conquest: Lodi Dynasty, 1451-1526.**—Tartars and Afghans were fighting for dominion, and the Afghans got the mastery. A line of Afghan Sultans reigned at Delhi which is called the Lodi dynasty, but the Punjab and Hindustan were convulsed by civil wars and revolts, like those which have distracted Afghanistan for the last hundred years. Meanwhile the race for Constantinople was over: the Ottomans were masters of Byzantium; and the Turks or Moghuls of Central Asia were preparing to wrest India from the Afghans.

16. **Summary.**—Mohammedan conquest in India was inspired by religion. Mohammedan warriors were zealous for the destruction of Hindu temples and idols, and for the conversion of the Hindu people to Islam. Some converts were made, but the masses clung to their religion and caste. In the end the Hindus were permitted to remain as they were, but required to pay a tribute or poll-tax known as the jezya. The Mohammedans belonged to different races, such as Arabs, Turks, Persians, Afghans and Moghuls. They were acquainted with Europe and Africa, as well as Asia. They cultivated history, but only that of Mohammedan dynasties. Thus the history of the Mohammedan Sultans of India is told at wearisome length, whilst that of Hindu Rajas and Maharajas is lost or forgotten, or can only be dimly traced in old inscriptions and local traditions.

CHAPTER III.

SOUTHERN INDIA: RAJPUTS, 1350-1565.

1. Rajputs, or "Sons of Rajas."—2. Old Rajput Sovereignties: lack of History.—3. Rajput Kingdoms to the South of the Jumna: Modern Rajputana.—4. Semi-Mohammedan Conquest.—5. Outlying Kingdoms: Guzerat, Malwa, and Bundelkund.—6. Hindus of the Deccan: Mahrattas and Gonds.—7. Hindus of the Peninsula: Kanarese, Telugus, and Tamils.—8. Hindu Kingdoms of the Peninsula.—9. Aryan Civilization in the Deccan and Peninsula.—10. Rajputs and Kshatriyas: Hindu Council.—11. Mohammedan Conquest of the Deccan.—12. Mohammedan Empire in the Deccan.—13. Impending Conquest of the Peninsula.—14. Hindu Empire of Vijayanagar, about 1350-1565.—15. War of Two Hundred Years.—16. Four Sultans of the Deccan: Ahmednagar, Berar, Bijapur, and Golkonda, about 1500.—17. Decline of the Hindu Empire of Vijayanagar.—18. Decisive Battle of Talikota, 1565.—19. Summary.

1. **Rajputs, or "Sons of Rajas."**—The Rajputs, or "Sons of Rajas," are soldiers by birth. They claim to represent the Kshatriyas, the old military caste of India; to be descended from those Aryan warriors who conquered the Punjab and Hindustan in Vedic times. They are brave and chivalrous; eager to resent an affront; and ready to to go into exile or outlawry rather than submit to injustice or injury, real or imaginary.

2. **Old Rajput Sovereignties: lack of History.**—The Rajputs claim to be the kinsmen of their princes, but their traditions are misty. The romance

of their past is told by their own bhats or bards, but glimpses of the reality are given by foreigners. The Greeks who accompanied Alexander the Great tell something of Taxiles and Porus. Arab travellers and Chinese pilgrims in like manner tell something of kingdoms and empires. In the fourth century before Christ, a Hindu sovereign, named Chandra-gupta, reigned at Patna over a great empire on the Ganges; and in the following century his grandson, Asoka the Buddhist, reigned over an empire which extended to the Indus. Chandra-gupta has been identified with Sandrocottus, a Hindu prince who visited Alexander the Great in the Punjab, and afterwards married a daughter of Seleucus, founder of the Græco-Bactrian kingdom in Central Asia. A thousand years rolled away after Asoka but there was little change. In the seventh century of the Christian era a Hindu lord paramount of Hindustan and the Deccan, named Sila-ditya, summoned his vassal Rajas to celebrate the great festival of almsgiving on the "field of happiness" at the junction of the Ganges and Jumna. Later still, Mahmud of Ghazni, and Kutub-ud-din of Delhi, fought against Rajput confederacies in the Punjab and Hindustan. But the Rajput princes were conquered by the Mohammedans. They abandoned their homes at Delhi and Kanouj, and went away to the south of the Jumna with their kinsmen and vassals. Little is known of them beyond oral traditions which are being fast forgotten.

3. **Rajput Kingdoms to the South of the Jumna: Modern Rajputana.**—Three divisions of Rajputs settled down at Jeypore, Jodhpore, and Chitor, in the region known as Rajputana. This territory lies between the Jumna and Nerbudda rivers, and is bounded west and east by the desert of Sind and the river Chambal. The Rajputs, kings and thakurs, were

linked together by feudal ties. Each division had its own Raja, and each Raja had his own thakurs, or chiefs of clans. The Raja founded kingdoms whilst the thakurs became lords of manors and were bound to render military service to their sovereign in time of war. The Rajas in their turn owed allegiance to the Rana of Chitor as their suzerain or "overlord." The Rana claimed to be descended from the old imperial line of Ayodhya or Oudh, of which Rama, the avatar of Vishnu, was the human hero. But in spite of these feudal obligations, chiefs and princes often fought against each other for estates or thrones, or refused to obey an "overlord," or took up arms against him; and feuds and wars, divided estates and divided kingdoms, have been the curse of Rajputana from the remotest antiquity.

4. **Semi - Mohammedan Conquest.** — The Mohammedans never reduced the kingdoms in Rajputana as they did those in the Punjab and Northern Hindustan. Ala-ud-din besieged the great hill fortress of Chitor for twelve years, but the Rajputs would not surrender. At last the Rajputs performed one of those terrible sacrifices for which they were always famous. They burnt their wives and children alive on a funeral pile in one vast holocaust, and then rushed out to die, sword in hand, or escape to the Aravalli mountains.

5. **Outlying Kingdoms: Guzerat, Malwa, and Bundelkund.**—Rajputana was a natural fortress protected by desert and mountain; but the Rajputs sallied forth from time to time and founded principalities and chiefships on either side. Some settled in Guzerat and Kandeish on the south; others in Malwa to the eastward of the Chambal; and others in the hills and jungles of Bundelkund and the regions still further to the eastward. The

Mohammedans conquered part of Guzerat, Kandeish, and Malwa; but they never established a footing in Bundelkund, or in the hill regions beyond.

6. **Hindus of the Deccan: Mahrattas and Gonds.**—The Deccan, or "South," is an open plain or table-land set in a framework of mountains. On the north is the Vindhyan range, which bars it off from the Rajput kingdoms of Hindustan. On the west is the mountain wall of the Western Ghats or Ghauts, which cuts it off from the Indian Ocean. On the east is the low range of hills and jungles, known as the Eastern Ghats, which intervenes between the table-land and the Bay of Bengal. On the south is the Kistna or Krishna river, with its affluent, the Tunga-bhadra, which separate the Deccan from the Peninsula. The table-land of the Deccan is divided between Mahrattas and Gonds; but the Mahrattas were the latest settlers, driving the Gonds and aborigines towards the unhealthy jungles of the Eastern Ghats. The Mohammedan conquest was a blow to the Mahrattas. The cultivators of the plains submitted without a struggle; but the warriors fell back on the Western Ghats and maintained their independence in mountain fortresses in the region known as the Konkan. In a later generation cultivators and warriors became fused into one community.

7. **Hindus of the Peninsula: Kanarese, Telugus, and Tamils.**—The Peninsula extends from the river Kistna to Cape Comorin. Its face is much the same as that of the Deccan, namely, a western table-land and an eastern plain. The Western Ghats cut off the table-land from the coast of Malabar as in the Deccan; but in the Peninsula the Eastern Ghats form a wall which separates the table-land from the eastern plain. The table-land is known as Mysore and is occupied by the Kanarese-speaking

people, whilst further south the Malayalam-speaking people occupy the narrow tract between the Western Ghats and the Malabar coast. The eastern plain, stretching to the coast of Coromandel, is wrongly known as the Carnatic, and is occupied by the Telugu and Tamil-speaking peoples.[1] All these people—Kanarese, Malayalam, Telugus, and Tamils—are divided into castes and called Hindus.

8. **Hindu Kingdoms of the Peninsula.**—In ancient times the Peninsula was divided into little kingdoms, like those of ancient Greece or Palestine. In each kingdom there was a Raja and his barons, who were Rajputs or Kshatriyas. In each kingdom there was also a colony of Brahmans, who served as priests and religious teachers, and were often the temporal and spiritual advisers of the reigning Raja. But the masses of the population were non-Aryans; settlers from upper Asia who preceded the Aryans and spoke languages which were not Aryan.

9. **Aryan Civilization in the Deccan and Peninsula.**—The Deccan and Peninsula are famous in Hindu tradition as the scene of Rama's wanderings. He appears in the Ramayana as the protector of the Brahmans against the Rakshasas, and the destroyer of Ravana, the king of Lanka, or Ceylon. He is thus associated with the extension of Aryan civilization, and possibly of Aryan conquest, amongst the non-Aryan populations. But it is the Brahmans rather than Rama who are responsible for the introduction of the caste system amongst the non-Aryan

[1] The term "Carnatic" ought only to be applied to the country of the Kanarese-speaking on the western side of the Peninsula. It has however been wrongly applied by Europeans to the eastern plain occupied by Telugus and Tamils, where the Kanarese language is not spoken.

populations, and the promulgation of the spiritual worship of Vishnu and Siva in the place of the orgiastic worship of the non-Aryans; in other words, for the assimilation of so many different races, languages, and religions under the general head of Hindus.

10. **Rajputs and Kshatriyas: Hindu Council.**—The Rajas and barons of the Deccan and Peninsula may have been Kshatriyas without being Rajputs. When the Brahmans entered Southern India and divided the people into castes, they would naturally accept all existing Rajas and barons as Kshatriyas, whether Aryan or otherwise. A certain Maharaja of the South convoked a great Council of Brahmans and Kshatriyas to consider why the Hindus were defeated by the Mohammedans. The Brahmans said that it was the will of God and had been foretold in the sacred books. The Kshatriyas said that it was because the Mohammedans rode stronger horses and were better archers.

11. **Mohammedan Conquest of the Deccan.**—The Mohammedans were content with the conquest of the table-land. They did not scale the Western Ghats to drive the Mahratta mountaineers out of their precipitous fortresses in the Konkan. Neither did they force their way into the feverish hills and jungles of the Eastern Ghats to subdue the Gonds and aborigines of Gondwana. They planted the banners of Islam on the table-land of the Deccan as an outlying province of the Delhi empire; but when the Delhi empire was breaking up they revolted, and formed a separate Mohammedan kingdom under a line of princes known as the Bahmini or Bahmani Sultans.

12. **Mohammedan Empire in the Deccan.**—The Bahmani Sultans fixed their capital at Gul-

barga, more than a hundred miles to the south-east of Deoghur. Their dominion was environed by Hindus; Rajputs on the north, Mahrattas on the west, Gonds and Uriyas on the east, and Kanarese and Telugus on the south. It was reinforced by Mohammedans from the outside world: Arabs, Abyssinians, and Nubians from the Red Sea; Persians and Afghans from Western and Central Asia. So long as they formed a solid commonwealth they overawed the Hindus. But they were divided by religion and race: Turk against Persian, Sunni against Shiah. The difference was that the Sunnis believed in the succession of the four caliphs of Medina,—Abubakr, Omar, Othman, and Ali; whilst the Shiahs contended that Ali alone, the son-in-law of Mohammed, and his two sons, Hassan and Husain, by Fatima the daughter of the Prophet, were the rightful successors or caliphs.

13. **Impending Conquest of the Peninsula.**—For a while the Mohammedans of the Deccan were kept tolerably together by their wars against the Hindus of the Peninsula. The south presented irresistible attractions to both Sunnis and Shiahs. Treasuries of Hindu Rajas were overflowing with gold and jewels. Temples of Hindu gods were covered with plates of gold. Idols of gold were hung with necklaces, bracelets, and anklets of precious metals, or studded with diamonds, emeralds, rubies, and precious stones. The Mohammedan armies in the reign of Ala-ud-din had returned to Delhi loaded with infinite riches. The Bahmini Sultans might have conquered the Peninsula with ease, but for their religious broils, and for a great Hindu fortress which resisted all the assaults of the Mohammedans for more than two hundred years.

14. **Hindu Empire of Vijayanagar, about 1350-1565.**—As far back as the early years of the

fourteenth century the Hindu kingdoms of the Peninsula began to make common cause against the Mohammedans. The Raja of Telingana was the first to resist the tide of Mohammedan invasion, but his fortress at Warangal was taken by storm, and he himself was carried prisoner to Delhi. Then followed the revolt of the Mohammedan army of the Deccan and the establishment of the Bahmani empire. Another Raja of Telingana joined the Raja of Kanara or Mysore, and a huge fortress of rock and granite was built at Vijayanagar on the southern bank of the Tunga-bhadra river. It was impregnable to an Asiatic army. It became the metropolis of a Hindu empire which extended from the Bay of Bengal to the Indian Ocean. Henceforth the united kingdoms of Telingana and Kanara were merged in the empire of Vijayanagar, and the Maharajas of Vijayanagar were lords paramount over all the countries to the south of the river Kistna.

15. **War of Two Hundred Years.**—For more than two hundred years there were intermittent wars between the Sultans of the Deccan and the Maharajas of Vijayanagar. The slaughter on either side was the most appalling in recorded history. The contest between Islam and Hinduism was aggravated by wanton insults. The Sultan gave some musicians an order for money on the treasury at Vijayanagar, as though the Maharaja were his vassal. The Maharaja in revenge fell by surprise on a frontier fortress of the Sultan between the Tunga-bhadra and the Kistna, and slaughtered the garrison. The Sultan swore that he would put a hundred thousand Hindus to death; and he kept his vow, slaying the helpless villagers like sheep, women and children as well as men. Later on the Maharaja invaded the Deccan with his army of Hindus, and slaughtered thousands of villagers before he was driven back to the Penin-

sula. The Mohammedans were strong soldiers, good archers, and rode the best horses of Arabia, Persia, and Turkistan. The Kshatriyas may have fought to the death after the manner of Rajputs, but the masses of Hindus were helpless. The Mohammedans made havoc throughout the Peninsula, but they could not capture the city and fortress of Vijayanagar. At last both sides were troubled at the wicked slaughter of women and children. Peace was made, and it was agreed that for the future no women or children should be slain, although they might be carried off into slavery. This compact however was sometimes forgotten, and then the carnage was as horrible as ever.

16. **Four Sultans of the Deccan: Ahmednagar, Berar, Bijapur, and Golkonda, about 1500.**—So long as the Bahmani empire of the Deccan was ruled by one Sultan, the Mohammedans were more powerful than the Hindus and compelled the Maharajas of Vijayanagar to send a yearly tribute to Gulbarga. But about the beginning of the sixteenth century the Bahmani empire was broken up into five kingdoms, each under a separate Sultan, and the five Sultans began to make war upon each other. On the north were Ahmednagar and Berar; on the south were Bijapur and Golkonda. In the centre was a little kingdom named Bidur, which is lost in the general history. After this dismemberment, the Maharajas of Vijayanagar began to withhold their tribute and to defy the Mohammedans. They were strong enough to fight Bijapur and Golkonda, and the three others were too far away, and too much engaged in their own quarrels, to interfere in the wars on the banks of the Kistna and Tunga-bhadra.

17. **Decline of the Hindu Empire of Vijayanagar.**—Meanwhile, however, the Hindu empire

was weakened by plots and tragedies at Vijayanagar which used to be common in Hindu principalities. The Minister was plotting to supplant the reigning family and set up his own family in its room. He married his son Ram Rai to a daughter of the Maharaja. He put to death by assassination and otherwise all the male princes of the imperial house, except an infant and a lunatic. Finally, when the last sovereign died, he installed his son Ram Rai on the throne as Maharaja of Vijayanagar. But Ram Rai was doomed. He exasperated the barons by his pride and arrogance. He maddened the Sultans by insulting their religion and treating them as vassals. The barons rebelled and set up the infant as their Maharaja. The lunatic assassinated the infant, and seized the throne for himself, and threatened to make over Vijayanagar to the Mohammedans. The barons were thus forced to come to terms with Ram Rai. The lunatic fell by his own sword, and Ram Rai became once again Maharaja of Vijayanagar.

18. **Decisive Battle of Talikota, 1565.**—At this crisis four Mohammedan Sultans banded together for the destruction of Ram Rai. A decisive battle was fought at Talikota. Ram Rai was defeated and slain, and his head carried away as a trophy to Bijapur. The city of Vijayanagar was captured and plundered by the Mohammedans, and abandoned to beasts and birds of prey. The empire of Vijayanagar was broken up into kingdoms and the barons became Rajas. The Sultans returned to the Deccan without conquering the Peninsula. A new Mohammedan power had arisen in Hindustan under the name of the Great Moghul, who was destined to become the lord paramount of India.

19. **Summary.**—The wars between Mohammedans and Hindus in Northern India were short and decisive.

The Rajputs were driven out of their empire in the Punjab and Hindustan on the north of the river Jumna, and migrated to the region south of the Jumna, namely, Rajputana and Malwa, and the outlying territories of Guzerat and Bundelkund, all of which were included in the term Hindustan. The wars in Southern India between the Mohammedan Sultans of the Deccan and the Hindu Maharajas of Vijayanagar in the Peninsula lasted for more than two hundred years, namely, from 1350 to 1565. The struggle was not only prolonged but bloodthirsty in the extreme. The history is told by Ferishta, an enlightened Mohammedan of the sixteenth century, who flourished in the Deccan, and sought to tell the truth and deal equal justice to Mohammedan and Hindu. It contains, however, some of the ghastliest episodes of assassination and massacre that are to be found in the whole range of Oriental annals.

CHAPTER IV.

MOGHUL EMPIRE IN INDIA, 1526-1761.

1. Chenghiz Khan the Moghul, 1154-1226.—2. Timur, the Chagatai Tartar, 1336-1405.—3. Turks and Persians.—4.—Baber, the Chagatai Turk, 1526-1530.—5. Humayun, 1530 : Exile in Persia, 1540-55.—6. Akbar, the Maker of the Moghul Empire, 1556-1605.—7. Conquests of Akbar.—8. Jehangir and Shah Jehan, 1605-58 : Court Life in Cities.—9. Nomadic Life in Camp.—10. Fear of Rebellion.—11. Moghul Constitution : Military Grandees.—12. Land Revenue.—13. Viceroys or Nawabs.—14. Aurangzeb, the strict Mohammedan, 1659-1707.—15. Conquest of the Deccan and Carnatic : Hindu Kingdom of Mysore.—16. Law and Justice.—17. Decline of Moghul Sovereignty at Delhi, 1707-38.—18. Growing Independence of Nawabs of Provinces.—19. Nadir Shah, 1738-39 : Massacre at Delhi.—20. Downfall of the Moghul Empire, 1739-48 : growing power of the Mahrattas.—21. Mahrattas crushed at Paniput, 1761 : Afghans masters at Delhi.—22. Summary.

1. **Chenghiz Khan the Moghul, 1154-1226.**—The new conquerors of India claimed to be descended from Chenghiz Khan the Moghul, and after him from Timur the Tartar. Chenghiz Khan was a demi-god of the northern steppes ; a hero of the howling wilderness of Gobi, or Shamo. He founded a kingdom over the Moghul Tartars, and henceforth they were the royal or ruling tribe in Asia. He created armies of Tartars, and conquered Northern China, Central Asia, Persia, and Eastern Russia, but he never invaded India. At his death he divided his vast empire amongst his four sons ; and one of these sons, named Chagatai Khan, inherited Central Asia, which

was nearest to India, and gave it the name of Chagatai. Chagatai proper was the region between the Jaxartes and the Oxus, but it probably included Khokand, Bokhara, Khiva and Kabul. Its capital was at Samarkand in Bokhara.

2. **Timur, the Chagatai Tartar, 1336-1405.**—Timur was a Chagatai Tartar claiming descent from Chenghiz Khan. He became master of Central Asia, and fixed his head-quarters at Samarkand. He overran Persia, Eastern Russia, Northern India, and Asia Minor, as already described (Chap. II., § 13). After his death in 1405 the empire was broken up by wars for the mastery, which lasted a hundred years. At length, about 1500, Persia became a separate monarchy under the Sufi Shahs, and Central Asia was conquered by a young Turk, named Báber, who rose to power at Samarkand in Bokhara, and afterwards at Kábul in Afghanistan.

3. **Turks and Persians.**—The names of Tartar and Turk have been indiscriminately applied to innumerable nomad tribes, speaking different tongues and widely distinct from each other. The Northern Tartars are yellow-complexioned, whilst the Southern Tartars are brown, black, and olive. The bulk have high cheek bones, flat noses, small eyes, and large mouths, denoting a Turanian or non-Aryan origin. But some tribes belong to a higher type, with commanding features and Aryan institutions. The Tartars proper are ignorant barbarians, superstitious and childlike; but the ruling Moghuls are arrogant and domineering. In the steppes Tartars and Moghuls live in tents of felt, and wear sheepskins and heavy boots. They will eat the flesh of a bird, beast or reptile, clean and unclean; rye bread as hard as stone, and cheese as tough as leather. They drink strong mead, fermented mares' milk called kumiss, and a black intoxicating

spirit made from grain. As they went south they accepted Islam, and were nicer in their eating, abstaining from impure meat as ordered by the Koran, and feasting on mutton and horseflesh, with boiled rice, wheaten bread, butter, cream, and sugar. They wore woollen tunics instead of sheepskins, and buskins instead of boots. They lost the hardy physique of the steppes, but their faces became oval, their complexions paler, and their features handsomer. Still further south they dwelt in cities, and appeared in long robes, flowing gowns, and loose sandals. In a word, they became Turks and Persians. In the present day, all Indian Mohammedans with fair complexions, excepting perhaps Afghans, are called Moghuls, whatever may have been their fatherland or mother tongue.

4. **Baber, the Chagatai Turk, 1526-1530.**—Baber, the founder of the Moghul empire in India, was a Chagatai Turk or Tartar. He was born in 1482. At the age of twelve he inherited the kingdom of Khokand on the Jaxartes. At sixteen he conquered Bokhara, and reigned at Samarkand. At twenty-three he crossed the Oxus, and founded a new kingdom in Kabul. In 1525-26, at the age of forty-four, he invaded the Punjab and Hindustan; defeated the Afghan Sultan near Delhi, and then advanced towards Agra and defeated the Rajput princes under their overlord, the Rana of Chitor. He spent the remaining years of his life in rooting Afghan chiefs out of their strongholds, and establishing his supremacy as sovereign or Padishah. He died in 1530, and was succeeded by his son Humayun.

5. **Humayun, 1530: Exile in Persia, 1540-55.**—Humayun was a prince of less capacity than Baber. He was outwitted by Shere Khan the Afghan, who held Bengal and Behar, and feigned submission to his authority. Humayun went away

to conquer the provinces of Guzerat and Malwa, which were the great outlets or highways from Hindustan into the Deccan. On returning to Agra he found that Shere Khan had thrown off his allegiance and become Sultan of Bengal and Behar. He marched an army against Shere Khan, but lost it in the defiles of the Rajmahal hills. He fled to Persia for refuge, and remained there fifteen years in exile. In 1555 he returned to Delhi with a Persian army, and recovered his sovereignty as Padishah, and might have recovered his empire, but was killed by a fall from a tower.

6. **Akbar, the Maker of the Moghul Empire, 1556-1605.**—Akbar, the son of Humayun, was the real maker of the Moghul empire. He conquered the princes of Rajputana, took their armies into his pay, raised them to high rank in his court, and bound them to his side by marrying their daughters. The Rana of Chitor stubbornly rejected his terms; abandoned his capital at Chitor; built a stronger city at Oodeypore, in the Aravalli hills; and refused to pay homage to Akbar, or to give him a daughter in marriage. Akbar employed his Rajput feudatories in conquering the Afghans, reducing all refractory Mohammedans, and throwing off the restraints of the Mohammedan religion. He married as many wives as he pleased, and tolerated all religions, to the disgust of the Mohammedan divines and lawyers, who wanted him to obey the Koran and persecute unbelievers. He claimed to be an incarnation of the Sun like Rama of Ayodhya; and he expected his subjects to worship him, whilst he himself publicly worshipped the Sun at its rising.

7. **Conquests of Akbar.**—Within a long reign of half a century, Akbar conquered Kabul and Kashmir on the north-west, and Behar and Bengal on the

south-east. He delivered India from the terror of the Afghans. He reduced the Mohammedan kingdoms of Guzerat, Malwa, and Kandeish, and converted them into Moghul provinces, thus opening a way from Hindustan into the Deccan. He overawed the Rajput princes by founding the Moghul province of Ajmere half-way down the Aravalli hills in the very heart of Rajputana. He threatened the Sultans of the Deccan, and conquered half the territories of Ahmednagar and Berar. But Bijapur and Golkonda were beyond his reach; and so long as these two kingdoms maintained their independence, the Great Moghul was barred out of the Peninsula.

8. **Jehangir and Shah Jehan, 1605-58: Court Life in Cities.**—Jehangir and Shah Jehan, the son and grandson of Akbar, reigned in succession over the new empire. They were not good men, for Jehangir was a drunkard, and Shah Jehan was notorious for vice and vanity. Outwardly they were better Mohammedans than Akbar, but they would not submit to the restrictions of the Koran. They were powerful sovereigns, and maintained the prestige of the empire without extending it. They lived in Tartar fashion softened by Persian luxury. Their cities were like camps; full of people when the Padishah was there, but empty and desolate when he went away. Every morning the Padishah showed himself in public, attended by his grandees, and received petitions, each accompanied by a present. At noon he sat in state; paraded troops, horses, camels, and elephants; and looked on gladiators, wrestlers, and the fighting of men with tigers and other animals. In the afternoon there was a public audience known as a durbar; there the Padishah received ambassadors, transacted public business, and condemned rebels and brigands to death in his presence. At evening there were select assemblies of ministers and grandees within the

palace, none being received but those expressly invited for the occasion.

9. **Nomad Life in Camp.**—The old nomad instinct was almost as strong in the Moghul rulers of India as in the so-called Chams of Tartary, the famous Chenghiz Khan and his sons and grandsons, as described by Father Rubruquis and Marco Polo. They made imperial progresses from city to city; from Delhi to Lahore and Kashmir on the north-west, and from Delhi to Agra, Ajmere, the Nerbudda river on the frontier of the Deccan, and the port of Surat still further south near the mouth of the river Tapti. From Hindustan to the Himálayas in the hot season, from Hindustan to the Deccan in the cold season, the Great Moghul was marching or halting with his wives and ministers, his grandees and armies, and vast trains of artizans, shop-keepers, and camp-followers. The Moghul camp was a moving city, with palaces and fortifications of imperial scarlet and gold in the centre; pavilions of white and blue for the grandees at fixed distances; streets of tents in regular order, and bazaars supplied with provisions and necessaries from all the villages round. When horse and foot, elephants, camels and mules, were on the march, burning incense was carried before the Padishah as though he were a god. The water of the Ganges was brought in jars, sometimes at long distances, for his special drinking. The cares of state were thrown aside, and hunting expeditions with lords and ladies took the place of the durbars.

10. **Fear of Rebellion.**—But whether in city or camp there was constant fear of rebellion. A son of the Padishah might rise against his father and make a desperate fight for the throne; and whenever a Padishah died, or was about to die, the sons made war upon each other for the succession until all were

slain, or shut up in hopeless captivity, or driven into helpless exile, except a single survivor, who secured the empire.

11. **Moghul Constitution: Military Grandees.**—The Moghuls had no feudal nobles with hereditary estates, such as existed amongst the Rajputs. They brought with them family titles, such as Khan and Mirza, but nothing that denoted landed property. The Padishah was the lord of the lives, liberties, and lands of all his subjects. There was no rank, office, or estate that might not be given or taken away at the will of the Padishah, who was the heir of his grandees, confiscating their property when they died, and making such provision as he thought proper for the widows and children. Honorary titles might be given to favoured individuals, denoting loyalty, valour, or piety, but the only rank was military command. This command ranged from one or two hundred horse to four or five thousand, for which either a monthly sum was paid out of the treasury, or the land revenues of certain villages were assigned under the name of jaghir. Princes, Viziers, Nawabs, and officers who were entrusted with local or special military services, were rewarded with army rank, and paid in like manner, until salaries were stopped or jaghirs were resumed.

12. **Land Revenue.**—The revenues of the Great Moghuls were mainly derived from the land. The Padishah claimed to be the proprietor of the soil, and to exact one-third of the gross yearly out-turn as rent. A Brahman, named Todar Mal, was appointed by Akbar to measure and value the lands, estimate the average harvest, and fix the rents. The story of the settlement is obscure; the work seems to have been completed in Moghul Hindustan but not in

Bengal and other outlying provinces. It was not perhaps so favourable to the ryots as in Rajput kingdoms, where the thakurs or barons held their lands as military fiefs, and exacted military service from the villagers. It was however more favourable to the ryots than in Hindu kingdoms of later date, where half the harvest, and often much more, was collected by the officials, and the cultivators and their families were left to starve.

13. **Viceroys or Nawabs.**—The Moghul empire was divided into fifteen or sixteen provinces. Each province was governed by a Nawab who commanded the local force, and was responsible for the public peace. In each province there was also a Dewan or Treasurer, who received the revenues and controlled the expenditure, and was not responsible to the Nawab, but only to the Padishah. The orders of the Padishah were paramount throughout the empire. Nawabs and Dewans were moved at his will from one province to another, or summoned to Court and rewarded with titles and jaghirs, or condemned to death and deprived of all their possessions.

14. **Aurangzeb, the strict Mohammedan, 1659-1707.**—Aurangzeb, son of Shah Jehan, was the last of the really Great Moghuls, and the one best known to Europeans. He abandoned the toleration of Akbar, and the laxity of Jehangír and Shah Jehan, and was a strict Mohammedan himself, and laboured to establish Islam as the state religion of India. He is said to have been a hypocrite, and certainly his career reveals the worst cruelties and crimes of Moghul times. He gained the throne at Delhi by wars and treacheries in which his brothers were slain, and his father, Shah Jehan, was imprisoned for life in the fortress at Agra. He reigned for half a century, but

was in constant fear that one or other of his sons would rebel against him. He completed the conquest of the Deccan by capturing Bijapur and Golkonda; and he put both the Sultans to death, declaring that they were Shiahs and heretics, whilst he himself was a Sunni.

15. **Conquest of the Deccan and Carnatic: Hindu Kingdom of Mysore.**—Henceforth the Deccan was formed into a separate province under the rule of a Viceroy, who was known as the Nizam; but the western frontier was exposed to the assaults of the Mahrattas of the Western Ghats, who had founded an independent dominion in the mountains, which was known as the kingdom of the Konkan. Further south, the eastern plain of the Peninsula, known as the Carnatic, was formed into a minor province subordinate to the Nizam, and placed in charge of a Nawab. The western table-land was still unconquered by the Mohammedans, and was ruled down to the latter half of the eighteenth century by the Hindu Raja of Mysore, a relic of the old empire of Vijayanagar.

16. **Law and Justice.**—The Great Moghul administered justice according to his own ideas of equity, possibly regulated by traditional laws handed down from Chenghiz Khan. Rebels, brigands, and river pirates were thrown to elephants to be tortured or trampled to death, or were hung or impaled by the side of roads or rivers, as warnings to evil-doers. Thieves and common offenders were flogged, fined, or deprived of an eye or arm. Under Akbar no execution was permitted without the order of the Padishah. Under Jehangir and Shah Jehan the rule was relaxed; but under Aurangzeb it was revived. Aurangzeb also introduced Mohammedan law in the

place of Moghul traditions, and this was the law of nearly all India down to modern times.

17. Decline of Moghul Sovereignty at Delhi, 1707-38.—After the death of Aurangzeb the Moghul empire began to decline. In splendour and prestige it was outwardly the same, but it was rotten at the core and losing its hold on the provinces. The Rajput princes were exasperated by the hostility of Aurangzeb towards their religion. They gradually withdrew from their dependence on Delhi and ceased to give their daughters in marriage to the Moghul. The successors of Aurangzeb degenerated into weak pageants, set up by rival ministers who were plotting against each other. The imperial progresses into the provinces were abandoned. The reigning Padishah was shut up in the palace at Delhi with wives and concubines, holding formal durbars, and occasionally going out to hunt with grandees and ladies, but always in mortal fear of assassination. All real authority was exercised by the minister who held the Padishah in tutelage. The Mahrattas had by this time grown into a predatory power which overawed half India. Their separate history will be dealt with in Chapter VI. For the present it will suffice to say that they were kept tolerably quiet by black mail or "chout," pronounced *chauth*, which amounted to about a quarter of the land revenue. Sometimes they appeared at Delhi as mercenaries to support some aspirant for power. At sunset the citizens of Delhi might be thrown into mortal terror by seeing the rude, half-clad, Mahratta horsemen picketing in the streets or keeping guard outside the palace. At sunrise next morning the thunder of kettledrums and roar of artillery might proclaim a new Padishah; the body of a murdered prince be carried off to be buried in the mausoleum of an emperor; and the Mahrattas would disappear from the city, to sell their services or seek fresh plunder in other quarters.

18. **Growing independence of Nawabs of Provinces.**—The Nawabs of provinces were as demonstrative as ever in abject submission to the Padishah, but were conspiring with the Dewans to keep back the revenue, and bribing the minister at Delhi to wink at defalcations. The Nawabs began to reign as kings. They were no longer moved about from one province to the other at the will of the Padishah, and when they died their sons intrigued or fought against each other for the succession. At this crisis Nadir Shah advanced with a large army from Persia to Delhi, and for a brief interval was the ruler of the destinies of India.

19. **Nadir Shah, 1738-39: Massacre at Delhi.**—Nadir Shah was a Turkish warrior of the type of Timur. He rose to power about 1730, when Persia was brought under Afghan rule. He pretended to help the Sufi Shahs against the Afghans, and then usurped the throne. He conquered all Persia and Afghanistan from the Turkish frontier on the river Tigris to the Moghul frontier on the river Indus. The passes through the mountains between Kabul and the Punjab were open to his advance. The Hill tribes who were paid to guard them had abandoned their posts, for they could not get their money from Delhi because the minister pocketed it. Nadir Shah entered Delhi as master. In the night the citizens fell on the Persian soldiery. Next morning Nadir Shah ordered a general massacre of the inhabitants, and watched the slaughter from a little mosque which is standing to this day. Eventually, Nadir Shah returned to Persia with money and jewels of the estimated value of a hundred millions sterling.

20. **Downfall of the Moghul Empire, 1739-48: growing power of the Mahrattas.**—The Moghul empire never recovered the blow. There was no money in the imperial treasury, and the Mahrattas were balked of their chout. One horde began to ravage the Carnatic, whilst another desolated Bengal, until the Nawabs of those provinces engaged to pay chout for the future. In a word, the Moghul empire was crumbling away before the assaults of the Mahrattas. Meanwhile, the Nawabs kept back the revenues of the provinces, and the government at Delhi was powerless to punish or interfere.

21. **Mahrattas crushed at Paniput, 1761: Afghans masters at Delhi.**—At this crisis the Afghans threatened to recover their empire in India. Nadir Shah was assassinated in 1747, and one of his Afghan generals, named Ahmed Shah Abdali, became king of the Afghans and conqueror of the Punjab. Afghans and Mahrattas were soon fighting for the supremacy at Delhi. In 1761, the Mahrattas were almost crushed at Paniput near Delhi. Most of their leaders were slain or wounded, and nearly 200,000 fell in battle, or were kept as prisoners and slaughtered in cold blood the morning afterwards. For a while Mahratta prestige was lost in Hindustan. A few shattered fugitives retreated southwards towards the Nerbudda river, and nothing but weeping and wailing were to be heard in the homes of the Mahrattas.

22. **Summary.**—The history of the Moghul empire in India is a relief after the cruel wars between Mohammedans and Hindus. The Moghuls were content to be conquerors, and were not fired by any zeal for the extension of Islam. Neither Akbar, nor Jehangír, nor Shah Jehan cared to convert the Hindus, or force them to become Mohammedans. Akbar

abolished the jizya, or poll tax on unbelievers in Islam, and neither Jehangír nor Shah Jehan cared to revive it. On the contrary, they entertained Brahmans and inter-married with Rajput princes. With Aurangzeb the case was different. He was lax in his marriages, but otherwise bent on bringing all India under the rule of Islam. He revived the hateful jizya, or poll tax, and exacted it from all who refused to become Mohammedans. He gloried in the conversion of Brahmans and Rajas. He persecuted those who rejected Islam, and rewarded those who embraced it. After his death, the Moghul empire wasted away from atrophy within and assaults from without. Thirty years after his death it was broken up by the invasion of Nadir Shah, and henceforth became a bone of contention between Afghans and Mahrattas.

CHAPTER V.

BRITISH SETTLEMENTS IN INDIA, 1600-1761.

1. Yearnings of London Merchants for Trade with India.—2. Portuguese Pioneers.—3. Dutch Carriers.—4. European Stories of the Great Moghul.—5. East India Company, 1600: Surat, 1612, Bengal, 1640.—6. Town and Fortress at Madras, 1639.—7. Island and Castle at Bombay, 1661-68.—8. Hooghly to Calcutta, 1690.—9. Surat to Bombay, 1700–1750.—10. Three Presidency Towns: Madras, Bombay, and Calcutta.—11. Peace in British Settlements, 1707–44.—12. War with France: Madras and Pondicherry, 1744.—13. Madras Captured by a French Fleet, 1746–48.—14. Dupleix, Governor of Pondicherry: triumphant in the Carnatic, 1748-51.—15. Clive recovers the Carnatic, 1751-52.—16. Dupleix's last hold in the Deccan: abandoned and ruined, 1752–55.—17. Seven Years' War, 1756-63: death of Ali Verdi Khan, Nawab of Bengal, April 1756.—18. Suraj-ud-daula captures Calcutta: Black Hole disaster, June 1756.—18. Recapture of Calcutta: Battle of Plassy, June 1757.—19. Mir Jafir, Nawab of Bengal, old and helpless, 1757-60.—20. End of the Seven Years' War in India, 1758-61.—21. Mir Kasim, Nawab: Peace with the Country Powers, 1760-61.—22. Summary.

1. **Yearnings of London Merchants for Trade with India.**—In the reign of Queen Elizabeth, the contemporary of Akbar, the merchants of London were longing for a share of the trade in the Eastern seas. They had read of the gold, jewels, and spices of Ophir; of the ivory, apes, and peacocks of Tarshish; of the Portuguese who discovered the passage round the Cape of Good Hope; and of British explorers who were seeking for a north-west passage through the Arctic seas. But they were sober-minded

traders, satisfied with London, and content to buy such Indian products as pepper and calicoes from the plodding Dutchmen on the Thames. Suddenly their wrath was kindled against the Dutch; the price of pepper was raised from 3*s*. to 6*s*. a pound; and they resolved to send ships of their own to the Eastern seas.

2. **Portuguese Pioneers.**—Portugal had forestalled the English by a hundred years. Before the dawn of the sixteenth century, before the Moghuls conquered Hindustan, and long before the Sultans of the Deccan conquered the Maharajas of Vijayanagar, the Portuguese had ruined the old route through Egypt and the Red Sea, and become masters of the trade round the Cape between Europe and India. Throughout the sixteenth century they held the monopoly of that trade against all comers from Europe. They built the city of Goa on an island off the coast of Malabar, and made it their metropolis in the East. They built factories and fortresses along the same coast from Guzerat to Cape Comorin. They built a smaller city at St. Thomé on the coast of Coromandel, where St. Thomas was said to have been martyred in apostolic times, and where Christians and Saracens were going on pilgrimage in the days of Marco Polo. They opened a trade with Bengal and Burma. They captured the town of Malacca and opened a trade with China and Japan. Meanwhile all other European nations were barred out of the Eastern seas; and no English or Dutch ship could attempt the voyage without the certainty of a desperate sea-fight with the Portuguese.

3. **Dutch Carriers.**—For generations the Dutch had been the carriers of Europe. They bought and sold at every market from the Mediterranean to the Baltic, and Amsterdam was an emporium. Every

year they went to Lisbon to buy Indian commodities of the Portuguese for re-sale at London and elsewhere. In 1580 they revolted against Spain, and were shut out of Lisbon. Henceforth they went to India for what they wanted; but, unfortunately, they doubled the price of pepper, and lost the custom of the disgusted Londoners who founded an East India Company of their own in order to follow the Dutch example.

4. **European Stories of the Great Moghul.**—British rovers and runaways however had found their way to India as early as the reign of Akbar. Some entered his service as gunners and workers in brass and iron. The Great Moghul on his part was as eager as Peter the Great to learn all he could of ships, cannon, and fortification. Meanwhile tales of his elephants, wives, menageries, fortresses, vast armies and enormous revenues, were told in London taverns. A crazy Englishman, named Tom Coryat, took an oath at the sign of the Mermaid in Bread Street, that he would go to India, see the Great Moghul and ride on an elephant. He fulfilled his vow by walking on foot from Jerusalem to Delhi, and so on to Ajmere, where the Great Moghul was holding his court in the heart of Rajputana. By this time Akbar was dead, but Coryat rode on an elephant and saw the Emperor Jehangír.

5. **East India Company, 1600: Surat, 1612, Bengal, 1640.**—The East India Company was formed in London in 1599. Next year it obtained a Charter from Queen Elizabeth for the monopoly of all trade between England and India. Ships were sent round the Cape, and returned to the river Thames after many a desperate battle with the Portuguese, but with cargoes that paid for all wounds and losses. In 1612 an agency house for buying and selling was established at Surat, about 200 miles to the north of

Bombay, the great port for pilgrim ships between India and Mecca. An ambassador, Sir Thomas Roe, was sent from James I. to the Emperor Jehangír, and secured special privileges for the traders in the service of the Company. Later on an English doctor from Surat healed the burns of a daughter of Shah Jehan whose dress had caught fire, and secured permission for the East India Company to trade in Bengal. The English founded a factory in the native town of Hooghly on the river of the same name, and sent cargoes of cottons and muslins to Europe. Then the civil war broke out between Charles I. and his Parliament, and the Company made large profits out of the saltpetre at Patna, which was wanted for gunpowder by the rival parties.

6. **Town and Fortress at Madras, 1639.**—The English, however, were not comfortable in the territories of the Moghul. They were not able to fortify their factories or to land cannon. When Aurangzeb was seated on the throne they suffered much from the oppressions and exactions of his Nawabs. Whenever disputes arose with a Nawab, the agency house at Surat, or the factory at Hooghly, would be environed by armed troops, and kept without provisions or necessaries until the English agreed to pay some heavy fine or ransom. They wanted factories and manufacturing towns outside Moghul dominion. In 1639 the English built a fortress at Madras, in Hindu territory, on the coast of Coromandel, hard by St. Thomé. They mounted it with cannon, and called it Fort St. George. In time it was strong enough to defy the Sultan of Golkonda, the Great Moghul, or the Mahrattas. A town grew up close beside it with a large population of weavers, artisans, brokers, bazaar dealers and others, mostly Hindus, who supplied the Company with goods and depended more or less upon the English for their livelihood.

7. **Island and Castle at Bombay, 1661-68.**—In 1661 King Charles II. received the island of Bombay from the Portuguese, with free trade of the English to the East Indies, as part of the dowry of his queen, Catherine of Portugal. It was situated off the Mahratta coast, between Surat and Goa, and was out of the reach of the Moghul. It proved however useless and costly to King Charles, and in 1668 was made over to the East India Company. The harbour is the largest in India, and open to all the trade of Persia, Arabia and Africa. Bombay Castle, built by the Portuguese, was strengthened with ramparts and cannon and made impregnable to any Asiatic force by sea or land. But the island was pestilential from salt marshes. The settlement was inside the harbour, and shut out from the breezes of the Indian Ocean by dense plantations of cocoa-nut trees manured by rotten fish. How the Portuguese lived there was a marvel. The sea-breeze, so pleasant at Madras, was loaded at Bombay with a tainted atmosphere which was deadly to English constitutions.

8. **Hooghly to Calcutta, 1690.**—In 1689 the English in Bengal were so oppressed by the Nawab that they would bear it no longer. They left Hooghly with all their goods and records and sailed to Madras. Then followed a change of Nawabs. The new ruler invited the English back again, and permitted them to rent three native villages on the northern bank of the river Hooghly, and twenty-five miles nearer the sea than their old factory. The villages were named Sutanati, Govindpore and Kali-ghat, and formed the nucleus of old Calcutta. A factory was built near the water's edge, which, in process of time, was strengthened with walls and guns, and known as Fort William.

9. **Surat to Bombay, 1700-1750.**—The English thus held three fortresses in India, namely, Fort St.

George, Bombay Castle, and Fort William. It was however a long time before they moved from Surat with its healthy breezes to Bombay with its deadly malaria. In the eighteenth century Bombay was cleared of cocoa-nuts and salt marshes, and has become in the nineteenth century one of the healthiest cities in India. Meanwhile, Surat gradually lost its importance, and Bombay became the centre of maritime trade.

10. **Three Presidency Towns: Madras, Bombay and Calcutta.**—Madras, Bombay and Calcutta, were known as Presidency towns because each one was the head of a group of factories. Each had a President or Governor, and a Council of four, namely, the head accountant, head warehouseman, head paymaster on land and head paymaster of shipping. Chiefs of factories, when at the Presidency, were also members of Council. The Governor and Council were supreme over the Presidency and its subordinate factories. They administered laws and collected taxes without interference from any potentate in India, and under the sole control of the Court of Directors of the East India Company in London. Madras and Bombay faced the sea. Madras commanded the factories on the coast of Coromandel, and Bombay those on the coast of Malabar. Calcutta and its factories were mostly inland, being connected by waterways which are numerous in Bengal. Calcutta itself was on a river a hundred miles from the sea. One factory was at Dacca, the old capital of Bengal; another at Kasimbazar (or Cossimbazar) near Murshedabad, the new capital; a third at Patna, the capital of Behar, four hundred miles up the Ganges; besides others of less note.

11. **Peace in British Settlements, 1707-44.**—Aurangzeb died in 1707 in the reign of Queen Anne.

After his death the British settlements were tranquil. In 1738-39 Nadir Shah invaded the north-west. Later on the Mahrattas plundered the Carnatic and Bengal provinces, but they never attacked the British fortresses. In Calcutta the British began to dig a ditch to keep out the Mahrattas, but it was never finished. Wild alarms might be going on outside the British settlements, but inside was always peaceful and orderly.

12. **War with France: Madras and Pondicherry, 1744.**—Suddenly the peace was broken by a war between Great Britain and France, which had nothing to do with India. The English at Madras were peaceful traders, and so were the French at Pondicherry, a hundred miles further south; and the two towns might have kept the peace towards each other in spite of the quarrel between the two nations. The Nawab of Bengal and the Nawab of the Carnatic, both declared that they would have no fighting in their provinces between European strangers.

13. **Madras captured by a French Fleet, 1746-48.**—In 1745, a British fleet from Europe appeared at Pondicherry, but the Nawab threatened to destroy Madras unless the ships sailed away. Next year a French fleet appeared at Madras, but the Nawab made no stir. He had received presents from the French to save Pondicherry, but none from the English to save Madras. The result was that Madras was bombarded and surrendered to the French, and the English inhabitants were carried off prisoners to Pondicherry. The war ended in 1748. Peace was proclaimed in Europe, and Madras was restored to the English in India.

14. **Dupleix, Governor of Pondicherry: triumphant in the Carnatic, 1748-51.**—In spite

of the peace in Europe war was soon renewed between Pondicherry and Madras. Dupleix, Governor of Pondicherry, was bent on founding a French empire in India. The Nawab of the Carnatic was killed. The English at Madras supported the claims of his son Mohammed Ali, but Dupleix set up a distant relation named Chunder Sahib in opposition. The Nizam of the Deccan died, and here again Dupleix supported a grandson against all rivals. By a clever stroke Dupleix brought his Nizam and Nawab to unite together against the English and their *protégé*. Mohammed Ali was driven out of his capital at Arcot, and closely besieged in the town of Trichinopoly. Had the French captured Trichinopoly, Mohammed Ali would probably have been put to death, Dupleix would have been master of Southern India, and the British would have lost all their settlements on the coast of Coromandel.

15. **Clive recovers the Carnatic, 1751-52.**—The French and their Asiatic allies were investing Trichinopoly when Robert Clive saved the East India Company from ruin. Arcot was open to attack as nearly all the garrison had gone to Trichinopoly. Captain Clive hurried with a small force to Arcot, and took the city by surprise. The French were thunderstruck at the loss of the capital, and compelled to raise the siege of Trichinopoly. The English were now triumphant in their turn. They enthroned Mohammed Ali at Arcot, while the Nawab set up by the French perished miserably.

16. **Dupleix's last hold in the Deccan: abandoned and ruined, 1752-55.**—Dupleix was defeated in the Carnatic but still triumphant in the Deccan. He set up a Nizam in Hyderabad, defended him against all enemies, and was rewarded by the cession of a large territory, known as the

Northern Circars, for the maintenance of a standing French army. But France did not want an army in the Deccan, and did not care for the Northern Circars. She listened to the enemies of Dupleix, who blamed him for the disasters in the Carnatic, and condemned him for his ambition in the Deccan. A new governor was sent to Pondicherry, and Dupleix returned to France and died in poverty. A peace was signed at Pondicherry in 1755, but it lasted only a few months. Great Britain and France were on the eve of the Seven Years' War.

17. **Seven Years' War, 1756-63: Death of Nawab of Bengal, April, 1756.**—Ali Verdi Khan, the Nawab of Bengal, Behar, and Orisas, died at Murshedabad in April, 1756. He had been a daring soldier in his younger days, but was worn out by the yearly incursions of the Mahrattas, and compelled to cede the greater part of Orissa, and to pay chout for Bengal and Behar. He left his throne to a grandson, named Suraj-ud-daula, who was proclaimed Nawab of Bengal, Behar, and Orissa, like his predecessors, but was threatened by rivals on all sides.

18. **Suraj-ud-daula captures Calcutta: Black Hole Disaster, June, 1756.**—The English in India were expecting the declaration of war against France. Those at Calcutta began to strengthen Fort William. The suspicions of the young Nawab were aroused, and he was told that one of his enemies had found refuge in Calcutta. In his wrath he arrested the English at the Kasimbazar factory, Warren Hastings amongst the number, and then marched from Murshedabad to Calcutta with an overwhelming army. The English fought desperately for five days and then surrendered Fort William. The prisoners, 146 in number, were thrown into a barrack cell within the Fort, known as the Black Hole. During the night

they were all suffocated, except twenty-three that were brought out half dead next morning.

19. **Recapture of Calcutta: Battle of Plassy, June 1757.**—A British force, under Colonel Clive and Admiral Watson, was despatched from Madras to Bengal. Calcutta was recaptured in January 1757, and in June the Nawab was utterly defeated by Clive in the famous battle of Plassy. A new Nawab, named Mir Jafir, was placed on the throne of Murshedabad, and the English might have quieted down to their trading pursuits at Calcutta but for the harassing war against the French which continued to disturb India.

20. **Mir Jafir, Nawab of Bengal, old and helpless, 1757-60.**—But India was breaking up. The Moghul government at Delhi was dying out. Mahrattas and Afghans were fighting for the supremacy. A son of the Moghul Padishah, known as the Shahzada, fled for his life to the court of the Nawab of Oudh; and the Nawab sent him with an army to demand possession of Bengal. Mir Jafir was old and helpless. Colonel Clive however defeated the Shahzada, and returned to England in 1760. But Calcutta, and the factories further inland, were threatened from all sides; and Clive recorded his conviction that unless a standing army of European soldiers and Asiatic sepoys was maintained under British officers, the East India Company must sacrifice the trade of a century, abandon their settlements in Bengal, and leave the richest province of India to become the prey of marauding armies.

21. **End of French War in India, 1757-61: sad fate of Lally.**—The war with France was over in India. In 1757 the French settlement at Chandernagore, near Calcutta, was captured by Clive

and Watson. In 1758 the French in the Deccan were driven out of the Northern Circars by a British force from Bengal. Count de Lally landed at Pondicherry the same year and besieged Madras, but was compelled to retire. In 1760 he was defeated by Sir Eyre Coote at Wandewash, and fell back on Pondicherry. In 1761 the French garrison at Pondicherry was starved into surrender. Lally returned to France and was imprisoned in the Bastille, and eventually executed to save the French government from the wrath of the French nation.

22. **Mir Kásim, Nawab: Peace with the Country Powers, 1760-61.**—After the departure of Clive, the English at Calcutta were alarmed lest Mahrattas or Afghans should find their way to Bengal. In January 1761 the Mahrattas were massacred by the Afghans at Paniput. The Moghul Padishah was murdered at Delhi. The Shahzada was still in Oudh ; he was proclaimed Padishah under the name of Shah Alam, and appointed the Nawab of Oudh to be his Vizier. Shah Alam and his honorary Vizier again threatened Bengal. The English at Calcutta saw that Mir Jafir could not protect the province, and set up another Nawab, named Mir Kásim, or Cossim, in his room. Mir Kásim, supported by the English, utterly routed Shah Alam and the Nawab Vizier. Terms were then arranged under which Mir Kásim was formally confirmed as Nawab of Bengal by the new Padishah, and was required to pay a yearly subsidy for the support of Shah Alam in Oudh territory.

23. **Summary.**—By this time the British were fast becoming the arbiters of India. The Afghans were masters at Delhi, but no one could tell whether they would return westward to Central Asia or advance eastward to the conquest of Oudh and Bengal.

The Mahrattas were groaning over their losses at Paniput. Meanwhile, an exiled Padishah was living in Oudh, under the protection of the Nawab Vizier. In Southern India the British were equally in the ascendant. They had set up Mohammed Ali as Nawab of the Carnatic and placed him on the throne at Arcot. They had driven French influence out of the Deccan, and occupied the Northern Circars. Finally, they had captured the city of Pondicherry, but restored it to the French at the close of the Seven Years' War under the treaty of 1763.

CHAPTER VI.

MAHRATTAS: BHONSLÁS AND BRAHMANS, 1627-1772.

1. Mahrattas of the Konkan.—2. Sivaji born near Poona, 1627: the "Mountain Rats" of the Deccan.—3. Plunder of Surat, 1664.—4. Moghul craft: Sivaji at Delhi.—5. Bombay Embassy to Sivaji, 1674.—6. Sivaji dies, 1680.—7. Princes and Priests: Bhonslás and Brahmans.—8. Mahrattas and Moghuls, 1680: Sahu Raja at Satara, 1707–48.—9. Brahman Ascendency: Rise of the Peishwas at Poona, 1748–61.—10. Gaekwar, Sindhia, Holkar and the Bhonsla.—11. Mahratta confederation after Paniput, 1761.—12. Mahdu Rao, Peishwa, 1761–72.—13. Relations with Bombay: Salsette and Bassein.—14. Relations with Bengal: demands for Chout.—15. Summary.

1. **Mahrattas of the Konkan.**—The Mahrattas are the only Hindus of modern times who have made a mark in history. They were an offshoot of the Rajputs. Whilst the Rajputs were kings of the Punjab and Hindustan, the Mahrattas went south, crossed the Nerbudda river, and entered the Deccan. Henceforth their homes were in the Western Deccan. Those on the table land were conquered by the Mohammedans of Delhi in the thirteenth century, and were eventually brought under the rule of the Sultans of the Deccan. Those nearer the sea were known as the Mahrattas of the Konkan, and became the Mahrattas of history. They were rude mountaineers who maintained a semi-independence in the Western Ghats, like that of the old Scotch or Welsh Highlanders. They came to the front in the seventeenth

century, when Aurangzeb was alarming the Hindus by his zeal for Islam. At this crisis a young Mahratta chief, named Sivaji, of the royal tribe of Bhonslás, created an army of mountaineers, who tilled the land for half the year, and engaged in war and pillage the other half. He plundered Hindus and warred against Mohammedans, whether from the north under the Moghul, or from the east under the neighbouring Sultans of the Deccan. Later on Sivaji conquered the Konkan from Surat to Goa, and became Maharaja of the Mahrattas, and the terror of the Deccan and Peninsula.

2. **Sivaji born near Poona, 1627 : the " Mountain Rats" of the Deccan.**—Sivaji was a bandit from his boyhood, and his exploits were those of a leader of bandits. He tempted a Mohammedan general of Bijapur into a lonely spot, and then murdered him with a treacherous weapon known as "tigers' claws." He would have assassinated an uncle of Aurangzeb, but the Moghul prince escaped through a window. His half-clad followers scoured the country on small Mahratta ponies with bags of grain at their sides, and harried and plundered the villages far and wide ; and then when threatened by regular troops they hurried back with all speed to burrow in their mountain fortresses. Aurangzeb, with his stately armies of cavalry, and trains of horses, camels, and elephants, looked with disdain on the Mahrattas, and called them the "mountain rats" of the Deccan. But he changed his note when the "rats" cut off his convoys of treasures and supplies, and carried off the spoil to their inaccessible fortresses.

3. **Plunder of Surat, 1664.**—The first experiences of the English were equally alarming. In 1664 Sivaji and his Mahrattas broke into the port of Surat and spent six days in plundering the city. The

Nawab was shut up in the fortress, whilst the inhabitants fled into the country. The English ordered up the sailors from the ships, and manfully defended the factory; and the Mahrattas were foiled in their repeated efforts to carry off the Company's goods and treasure.

4. **Moghul craft: Sivaji at Delhi.**—Aurangzeb tried to entrap Sivaji. He pretended to admire his exploits, and offered to make him Viceroy of the Deccan if he would come to Delhi and do homage. Sivaji swallowed the bait. He was dazzled by the prospect of power and plunder. He went to Delhi expecting to be received with honour and glory, but saw that he was held in contempt and that his life was in danger. He escaped from Delhi in a vegetable basket, and then disguised himself as a religious beggar. After months of hairbreadth escapes from the spies of Aurangzeb he reached the Deccan in safety. He waged war against Aurangzeb all the rest of his days.

5. **Bombay Embassy to Sivaji, 1674.**—Years passed away. Sivaji lost his hold on Poona. He fell back as the Moghuls advanced, and established his head-quarters at the strong fortress of Raighur, about thirty miles further south. In this fortress in the year 1674 Sivaji was installed with great ceremony as Maharaja of the Konkan. The English at Bombay sent ambassadors to congratulate him, and hard work they had to climb up the side of the fortress. It was a precipitous pile of rock with a narrow path to the top up which only one man could go at a time. Inside the fortress were cultivated fields where enough grain was harvested during the year to feed the whole garrison. Sivaji received the ambassadors graciously, and said he wished to promote commerce; but the English found it impossible to open out a

trade in the Deccan. The Mahrattas cared for nothing but war and plunder, and it was hazardous for either merchants or artisans to live in their territories.

6. **Sivaji dies, 1680.**—Later on Sivaji ravaged the Carnatic round about Madras, and planted a Mahratta kingdom further south in Tanjore. He died in 1680 at the age of fifty-three.

7. **Princes and Priests: Bhonslás and Brahmans.**—Mahratta history, like early English history, was marked by a rivalry between princes and priests; between the royal tribe of Bhonslás and the sacred caste of Brahmans. Sivaji was very much influenced by Brahmans. His Council consisted of eight Brahmans, and the head of the Council was premier or Peishwa. The officials who kept the accounts of revenue, chout, and expenditure were all Brahmans. After the death of Sivaji the Peishwa grew more powerful, but always professed the utmost subservience to the Maharaja.

8. **Mahrattas and Moghuls, 1680: Sahu Raja at Satara, 1707-48.**—Sivaji was succeeded by sons of less capacity and the history grows confused. The wars between Mahrattas and Moghuls continued till the death of Aurangzeb in 1707. Then followed a compromise. A grandson of Sivaji, known as Sahu Raja, had been taken prisoner as a child and brought up in the camp of Aurangzeb. He was placed on the throne at Satara, about sixty miles south of Poona, as a vassal Raja, owing allegiance to the Moghul. The Mahrattas were satisfied, as they were paid a nominal chout out of the treasury at Delhi. When the treasury was emptied by Nadir Shah, they collected chout in the Carnatic and Bengal provinces. Sahu was content with the title of Raja or Maharaja, and left the government to be carried on

by the prime minister, a Mahratta Brahman who founded the line of Peishwas. Sahu died in 1748.

9. **Brahman Ascendency: Rise of the Peishwas at Poona, 1748-61.**—During the reign of Sahu the office of Peishwa became hereditary. After the death of Sahu, his successor was shut up in the fortress at Satara, and the Peishwa removed to Poona and became sovereign. The old titles, however, were still kept up. The royal prisoner at Satara was still known as the Maharaja, and the Brahman minister at Poona, who exercised all the powers of sovereignty, was content with the humbler title of Peishwa.

10. **Gaekwar, Sindhia, Holkar and the Bhonsla.**—The Peishwa was thus king of the Konkan, and sovereign lord of the Mahratta confederacy. By this time Mahratta lieutenants were appointed to collect revenue or chout in Guzerat, Malwa, and Berar. Each lieutenant grew into a prince and called himself a Maharaja, but owed allegiance to the Peishwa. In Guzerat he was known as the Gaekwar. In Malwa there were two lieutenants, Sindhia and Holkar. In Berar the lieutenant was known as the Bhonslá, because he belonged to the same royal tribe as Sivaji.

11. **Mahratta Confederation after Paniput, 1761.**—The defeat of the Mahrattas at Paniput, as told in Chapter IV., § 21, paralyzed for awhile their power and prestige. It did not break up the confederation, but it loosened the ties which bound the lieutenants to the Peishwa. The reigning Peishwa died broken hearted. His son succeeded, a boy Peishwa, with an uncle for regent. The son was named Mahdu Rao. The uncle was Rughonath Rao, known to Europe as Ragoba. Mahdu Rao and his

uncle quarrelled. The four lieutenants—Sindhia and Holkar, the Gaekwar and the Bhonsla—ignored or defied the Peishwa. The Bhonslá of Berar, who belonged to the same royal tribe as Sivaji, intrigued with the Mohammedan Nizam of Hyderabad to supplant the Peishwa and become Maharaja by virtue of his kinship to the family of Sivaji.

12. **Mahdu Rao, Peishwa, 1761-72.**—The young Peishwa, Mahdu Rao, was environed by enemies whilst suffering from the hostility of his uncle Ragoba. On the south a new Mohammedan power was rising in the Mysore under Hyder Ali. On the east the Nizam of Hyderabad was threatening Poona. On the north the four lieutenants were plotting, scheming, and changing sides with bewildering rapidity. Eventually the uncle Ragoba was imprisoned in a fortress. Mahdu Rao invaded Mysore and wrested a large territory from Hyder Ali. He won over the Nizam from the Bhonsla of Berar, and converted him into an ally. He marched an army towards the north, crossed the Nerbudda river, menaced his refractory lieutenants, and collected chout from the princes and chiefs of Rajputana. In a word, under Mahdu Rao, the Mahratta power recovered from its losses at Paniput, and prepared to drive the Afghans out of Delhi. He died in 1772.

13. **Relations with Bombay: Salsette and Bassein.**—The Mahrattas generally kept aloof from the British. When they desolated the Carnatic and Bengal they might threaten Madras or Calcutta, but they never attacked either settlement. On the Bombay side the relations were closer. The British sent envoys to Sivaji in the hope of trade. They sent envoys to Mahdu Rao in the hope of buying Salsette and Bassein. The island of Salsette and the port of Bassein lay to the north of Bombay, and

belonged to the Portuguese. For a long time they formed a Portuguese barrier on the land side between the British and the Mahrattas. But in 1739 the Mahrattas conquered both places. Bombay was thus at the mercy of the Mahrattas. Henceforth the Governor and Council at Bombay, and the Directors of the East India Company in London, were passionately desirous of buying Salsette and Bassein, but the Mahrattas would not sell or cede them for any consideration that could be offered.

14. **Relations with Bengal: demands for Chout.**—Meanwhile the Mahrattas claimed chout for Bengal, Behar and Orissa from Nawab Ali Verdi Khan. For eight years, from 1742 to 1750, they desolated Bengal year after year until the old Nawab ceded the greater part of Orissa and engaged to pay a chout of £120,000 per annum for Bengal and Behar. The Bhonslá of Berar occupied Orissa but could not get the chout. Mir Jafir could not pay it; Clive would not; and the Directors in England scorned the idea. Accordingly the matter remained in abeyance.

15. **Summary.**—Mahratta history is divisible into four eras. First, the rise of Sivaji from the leadership of brigands to the throne of the Konkan. Second, the installation of his grandson Sahu at Satara, as a vassal Maharaja, paying homage to the Moghul. Third, the imprisonment of the Maharaja in the fortress of Satara, and the usurpation of the Brahman Peishwas at Poona. Fourth, the crushing defeat of the Mahratta confederation at Paniput, and temporary establishment of Afghan supremacy at Delhi.

CHAPTER VII.

BRITISH SUPREMACY IN BENGAL, 1761-65: LORD CLIVE DICTATOR, 1765-67

1. British Traders anxious for Peace.—2. Bengal: British supreme, 1761.—3. Quarrel with Mir Kasim, 1762.—4. Massacre at Patna: Ruin of Mir Kasim, 1763-64.—5 Defeat of Shah Alam and the Nawab Vizier at Buxar, 1764. 6. Death of Mir Jafir: Ruinous Policy, 1765.—7. Lord Clive, Governor, 1765-67: Nawab of Bengal and two Naibs.—8. Settles the Padishah and Nawab Vizier of Oudh. 9. Standing British Army of Bengal.—10. East India Company created Dewan of Bengal and Behar.—11. Success of Lord Clive's Administration, 1765-67.—12. Errors. 13. Complaints against Lord Clive.—14. Interval between Clive and Warren Hastings, 1767-72.—15. Flight of the Moghul Padishah to Delhi in charge of Sindhia.—16. Summary.

1. **British Traders anxious for Peace.**—The British in India were still merchants devoted to trade and anxious for peace and security. In both Bengal and the Carnatic they received the revenues of certain districts for the maintenance of troops for the support of the Nawab; but their aim was to protect their own settlements and leave the Nawab in each province to provide for the defence of his territories. In Bombay the British were shut up in their little island, carrying on their trade entirely by sea and watching the Mahrattas on the main land.

2. **Bengal: British supreme, 1761.**—In Bengal the British had set up a Nawab on their sole respon-

sibility. In Madras they had supported Mohammed Ali as a matter of right, because he was the son of the deceased Nawab. But in Bengal they installed Mir Jafir as a matter of interest and self-preservation; and when he proved a failure, they set up his son-in-law Mir Kásim.

3. **Quarrel with Mir Kasim, 1762.**—In Bengal the British quarrelled with Nawab Mir Kasim about the payment of inland transit duties. In making him Nawab they had claimed the privilege of carrying their goods duty free. Mir Kasim rendered the privilege of no value by extending it to all native dealers. Meanwhile Mir Kasim was preparing for war. He had removed from Murshedabad, 100 miles north of Calcutta, to Monghyr, 300 miles further west. At Monghyr he trained and drilled an army. A party of his soldiers murdered a British envoy who had been sent to Monghyr to settle the dispute. In revenge the British at Calcutta formally deposed him and set up old Mir Jafir in his room; and then sent an army to Monghyr to punish him for the murder.

4. **Massacre at Patna: Ruin of Mir Kasim, 1763-64.**—Mir Kasim was driven to madness by these proceedings. He captured the British factories on the Ganges, and sent 150 prisoners to Patna where they were brutally murdered by his orders. He then fled into Oudh with his treasures, but was despoiled of his money and jewels by the Nawab Vizier. He perished in obscurity, knowing that the British would never restore him, and that neither the Padishah nor the Nawab Vizier cared to support his cause except to carry out their own ends.

5. **Defeat of Shah Alam and the Nawab Vizier at Buxar, 1764.**—Later on the Padishah and Nawab Vizier marched an army towards Patna

to take possession of Behar and Bengal, but were utterly routed by the British in the famous battle of Buxar. The Padishah, Shah Alam, took refuge in the British camp, whilst the Nawab Vizier fled away to the north-west, and left his territories at the disposal of the Governor and Council at Calcutta.

6. **Death of Mir Jafir: Ruinous Policy, 1765.**—Early in 1765 Mir Jafir was dead. The British at Calcutta set up his son as Nawab of Bengal and Behar. They had been over-persuaded to send Shah Alam to Delhi under a British escort, and to make over Oudh to the Afghan power at Delhi. The last proceeding would have been rash and ruinous. At Delhi the British might have been overwhelmed and murdered. The Afghans would once again have been masters of Hindustan, and would have proved troublesome neighbours to the British in Bengal.

7. **Lord Clive Governor, 1765-67: Nawab of Bengal and two Naibs.**—At this crisis Lord Clive arrived from England with full powers. During his stay in England, or perhaps during his voyage out, he had decided to set up a Nawab of Bengal as a creature of the English, whilst securing the revenues for the East India Company. He accepted the son of Mir Jafir as the new Nawab, but found him helpless and foolish. Accordingly he appointed two Naibs or deputies to act for him; one a Mohammedan, named Mohammed Reza Khan, to govern Bengal Hindu, named from Murshedabad, and the other a Shitab Roy, to govern Behar from Patna.

8. **Sets up the Padishah and Nawab Vizier of Oudh.**—Lord Clive was furious at the proposal to send Shah Alam to Delhi and to make over Oudh to the Afghans. He was determined to set up Shah Alam as a puppet Padishah, and he purposed to keep him in Bengal. Shah Alam however refused to

accept any terms which would bar his possible return to Delhi. In the end it was arranged that Shah Alam should reside at Allahabad in Oudh territory, and be maintained by subsidies from Oudh and Bengal as his imperial share of the revenues of those provinces. At the same time Lord Clive restored Oudh to the Nawab Vizier, and of course dictated his own terms.

9. **Standing British Army of Bengal.**—Finally Lord Clive provided for the maintenance of a standing army of British soldiers and Indian sepoys under the command of British officers, such as he had contemplated before leaving Bengal in 1760, for keeping the peace in Bengal and Oudh, and shutting out Afghans and Mahrattas (see Chap. V. § 20). The Nawab Vizier of Oudh was required to furnish yearly a portion of the funds required, but the bulk was supplied from the revenues of Bengal.

10. **East India Company created Dewan of Bengal and Behar.**—Lord Clive took over all the revenues of Bengal, Behar, and part of Orissa in the name of the East India Company. The Company on its part was to pay salaries to the Nawab of Bengal and Behar for the support of his family and officials, and a salary to Shah Alam as his imperial share. The arrangement placed the surplus revenues of Bengal and Behar at the absolute disposal of the East India Company. It was covered up under Moghul forms. Shah Alam was assumed to be a real Padishah, with all the sovereign powers of an Akbar or Aurangzeb. The Nawab of Bengal and Behar was appointed in his name, and the East India Company was appointed to be Dewan or treasurer. This was called the grant of the Dewani, but in fact it was the surrender to the Company of the revenue and virtually of all sovereign

powers. Henceforth the Governor and Council at Calcutta disbursed the revenues, and commanded the army in Bengal under the control of the East India Company in London.

11. **Success of Lord Clive's Administration, 1765-67.**—The grant of the Dewani was regarded for a while as a grand success. Lord Clive was the political genius who had solved the problem of Bengal. There was no annexation, for a Nawab and a Great Moghul were supported out of the revenues. There was no interference with the native government, which was left to collect the revenue and make it over to the Company's servants, and to administer justice so long as prosecutors paid for it. Above all there was peace. There was no fear of Mahrattas or Afghans. A standing army of soldiers and sepoys, commanded by British officers, was maintained out of the revenues of Bengal, and sufficed for the defence of the country against any invading force, Asiatic or European.

12. **Errors.**—Before Lord Clive left India he was aware of the defects of his scheme. He had built it up on the *débris* of the Moghul system, without the old safeguards. There was no control, for Lord Clive would not be responsible for the native government, and the British would not interfere with the Asiatic officials. Padishah and Nawab were ciphers. The two Naibs exacted the revenues to the uttermost farthing, but paid as little as possible into the British treasury. Lord Clive appointed a British supervisor to every district, but with strict orders not to interfere with the native officials. Consequently nothing was done.

13. **Complaints against Lord Clive.**—The enemies of the East India Company bitterly re-

proached Lord Clive. The old charges were revived of his having received vast presents from Mir Jafir, but these were obvious rewards for his victory at Plassy, and no one could say that he was guilty of receiving bribes. But his mind gave way under repeated detractions, and he eventually perished by his own hand.

14. **Interval between Clive and Warren Hastings, 1767-72.**—After Lord Clive returned to England, Bengal was depopulated by famine and the revenue fell with alarming rapidity. Strong measures were necessary for restoring the old prosperity. The Directors were driven to desperation, and at last resolved to intrust the collection of the revenue of Bengal and Behar to their English civil servants.

15. **Flight of the Moghul Padishah to Delhi in charge of Sindhia.**—Meanwhile the sham of a Padishah was brought to a close. Shah Alam abandoned his dependence on the East India Company, and returned to Delhi under the escort of Mahadaji Sindhia. The daring Mahratta was bent on driving out the Afghan supremacy, and governing Hindustan in the name of the Great Moghul; and Shah Alam was eager to be restored to the throne of Akbar and Aurangzeb.

16. **Summary.**—Within ten years of the Black Hole disaster, the East India Company had become lords of Bengal and Behar. There are five distinct stages in this revolution. First, Clive's victory at Plassy and the installation of Mir Jafir. Second, the invasion of Shah Alam and his Nawab Vizier, and the installation of Mir Kasim. Third, the massacre at Patna and flight of Mir Kasim. Fourth, the decisive battle of Buxar, which placed Oudh as well as Bengal and Behar at the disposal of the British. Fifth, the second administration of Lord Clive.

CHAPTER VIII.

WARREN HASTINGS, GOVERNOR OF BENGAL, 1772: GOVERNOR-GENERAL, 1774-85.

1. British Collectors and Magistrates, 1772.—2. Warren Hastings, boy and man, 1732-56.—3. Political Experiences, 1756-64: Furlough to England, 1764-69.—4. Peace in Bengal, Bombay, and Madras, 1769.—5. Warren Hastings, Governor of Bengal, 1772-74: end of Nawab, Naibs, and Padishah.—6. Revenue Difficulties: Zemindari Auctions and Leases.—7. Administration of Justice.—8. Claim of the Nawab Vizier against the Rohillas.—9. British Campaign against the Rohillas, 1774.—10. Interference of Parliament with the Company's Administration, 1774.—11. New Supreme Court of Barrister Judges.—12. Philip Francis, the Enemy of Warren Hastings.—13. Trial and Execution of Nundkomar.—14. Bombay Longings for Salsette and Bassein.—15. Plots and Murders at Poona: Exile of Ragoba, 1774.—16. War with Poona: Stopped by Bengal, 1775-76.—17. War with France: First Mahratta War, 1778-82.—18. Genius of Warren Hastings: Duel with Francis.—19. War with France: Hostilities of the Nizam and Hyder Ali, 1778-82.—20. Hyder Ali invades the Carnatic, 1780-84: driven back by Sir Eyre Coote.—21. Parliamentary Interference: Board of Control, 1784.—22. Warren Hastings in England, 1785: Trial in Westminster Hall, 1788-94.—23. (1) Unjust Wars: Rohilla and Mahratta.—24. (2) Corrupt Receipt of Money.—25. (3) Demand on the Raja of Benares.—26. (4) Treatment of the Oudh Begums.—27. Results of the Trial.—28. Summary.

1. British Collectors and Magistrates, 1772.—The Court of Directors appointed Warren Hastings to be Governor of Bengal. They ordered him to remove the Nawab and two Naibs from all connection with the revenue. Asiatic rule faded away and British rule took its place. The British supervisors who had been appointed to the districts by Lord Clive were turned into collectors and magistrates. They received the revenue from the zemindars or renters, and administered justice in their room. Such was the origin of the collector-magistrates of British India.

2. **Warren Hastings, boy and man, 1732-56.**—Warren Hastings was well qualified for his important post. He had been educated at Westminster School, where he was known to Cowper the poet and other school-fellows as a mild and gentle boy. In 1750, at the age of eighteen, he went as a writer to Bengal. At first he was employed in the Secretary's office at Calcutta, where all proceedings and correspondence were recorded. In 1753 he was sent to the Kasimbazar factory, the centre of the silk industry, where he rose to be a member of the factory Council. The city of Murshedabad was hard by, where the old Nawab, Ali Verdi Khan, held his Court, and where Hastings must have learnt something of Moghul grandees and Mohammedan culture.

3. **Political Experiences, 1756–64: furlough to England, 1764–69.**—Warren Hastings was at Murshedabad when the old Nawab died and the young Nawab marched against Calcutta. After the battle of Plassy he resided there as representative of the British government at the court of Mir Jafir. In 1761, before he was thirty, he was a member of the Council at Calcutta, and tried to stop the quarrel with Mir Kasim, and showed himself better versed in public law and polity than any other Englishman in Bengal. In 1764, at the age of thirty-two, he visited England, and became acquainted with Dr. Johnson. In 1769, at the age of thirty-

seven, he returned to India as member of Council at Madras.

4. Peace in Bengal, Bombay, and Madras, 1769.—The British were now at peace in all three Presidencies. In Bengal, Lord Clive had put an end to all internal war. Outside Bombay the Mahrattas were recovering from the defeat at Paniput. At Madras there had been wars, but they were over. The Nizam of the Deccan and Hyder Ali of Mysore had each invaded the Carnatic and threatened Madras, but in 1769 peace was concluded with both powers, the British at Madras agreeing to help either the Nizam on the north or Hyder Ali on the west, in the event of war.

5. Warren Hastings Governor of Bengal, 1772-74 : end of Nawab, Naibs, and Padishah.—Warren Hastings reached Calcutta in 1772. He turned, as already seen, the supervisors into collector-magistrates. He deposed the Nawab and reduced his stipend. He put the two Naibs under arrest, which had been ordered by the Court of Directors, but afterwards released them for lack of judicial evidence. Later on Mahadaji Sindhia demanded the subsidies that Lord Clive had apportioned to the would-be Padishah. Warren Hastings refused payment. The subsidies had been granted to support the Padishah at Allahabad, not to support Sindhia at Delhi.

6. Revenue Difficulties: *Zemindari Auctions* and Leases.—The land revenue was the great stumbling-block to Warren Hastings. It had been collected from the ryots or cultivators by the zemindars or renters; but Warren Hastings could not learn what rents were paid by the ryots to the zemindars, and consequently he could not fix the revenue to be paid by the zemindar to the British collectors. The zemindaries or revenue estates were put up to auction, but the buyers became defaulters. At last rough valuations were made and leases were granted for fixed yearly payments, but there were many irregularities and corrupt collusions, as the native records were missing or falsified. Indeed it was impossible in those days, with the limited means which Warren Hastings had at his command, to undertake the work of a regular survey and settlement; namely to assess revenues and rents on actual measurements of fields and farms, and precise calculations of the average yearly values of crops.

7. **Administration of Justice.**—New courts of justice were created, but they were the work of years. British judges were appointed to go on circuit for the trial of criminals who had been committed to jail by the collector-magistrates, and for the settlement of civil disputes respecting property, inheritance, and such like matters. The Governor and Council sat at Calcutta as a High Court of Appeal in both criminal and civil cases, which was known for ninety years afterwards as the "State" Court or "Sudder."

8. **Claim of the Nawab Vizier against the Rohillas.**—Meanwhile the Nawab Vizier of Oudh persuaded Warren Hastings to send a British force against the Rohillas. These people were Afghan colonists, who had settled on the north-west frontier of Oudh, and were known as Rohillas or "mountaineers." They had been attacked by Sindhia's Mahrattas at Delhi, but got rid of them by promising to pay forty lakhs of rupees, or nearly half a million sterling. They next promised the money to the Nawab Vizier if he would keep off the Mahrattas. Suddenly Sindhia and his Mahrattas disappeared; they had been called away from Delhi by the death

of Mahdu Rao, Peishwa at Poona. The Rohillas refused to pay the money to the Nawab Vizier, and the Nawab Vizier promised to pay the amount to the East India Company if Warren Hastings would send a British brigade against the Rohillas.

9. **British Campaign against the Rohillas, 1774.**—Warren Hastings was sorely troubled. He saw that the Rohilla country would give the Nawab Vizier a strong frontier against the Mahrattas, but he feared that the expedition might be condemned in England. However the brigade was sent; the Rohillas were crushed; the British troops did all the fighting, and the Nawab Vizier's army carried off all the treasure.

10. **Interference of Parliament with the Company's Administration, 1774.**—Meanwhile the British Parliament interfered with the Company's rule in India. It confirmed Warren Hastings as Governor of Bengal, and made him Governor-General. Henceforth the Governor-General and Council at Bengal controlled Madras and Bombay in all matters of peace and war. Parliament sent three new members of Council of its own choosing to sit at Calcutta in place of those Company's members who were leaving the service. Warren Hastings was President, and one member of Council remained who had been appointed by the East India Company; so that the three new members had a majority of one, and could override the Governor-General. Their names were General Clavering, Colonel Monson, and Philip Francis.

11. **New Supreme Court of Barrister Judges.**—Parliament also created a new Supreme Court at Calcutta to administer English law and protect Asiatics. The new judges had been trained at

the English bar and were sent out from England. Sir Elijah Impey was Chief Justice, and three other barristers were Puisne judges. The Supreme Court was independent of the Governor-General and Council, and interfered in civil suits between Asiatics. Eventually its jurisdiction was confined to Europeans, and to Asiatics dwelling within the limits of Calcutta.

12. **Philip Francis, the Enemy of Warren Hastings.**—Philip Francis, one of the three new members of Council, became a bitter enemy of Hastings, and carried the other two with him. He condemned the Rohilla war. He listened to charges of corruption which were brought against the Governor-General by a Brahman of bad character named Nundkomar.

13. **Trial and Execution of Nundkomar.**—Nundkomar was tried in the Supreme Court at Calcutta for forgery, which in those days was punished by death under English law. He was found guilty, and suffered the extreme penalty. The execution of Nundkomar has been much debated. He was a Brahman, and the slaughter of a Brahman was regarded by Hindus as a sin. Forgery was not a capital offence in Asiatic eyes, but only under English law. The Supreme Court was accused of straining the law to gratify Hastings, but the charge has been investigated and refuted by Sir James Stephen. Since then the law has been altered, and criminals convicted of forgery are no longer punished by death in any part of the British empire.

14. **Bombay Longings for Salsette and Bassein.**—Meanwhile a storm was brewing at Bombay. It originated in the longings for Salsette and Bassein already described in Chapter VII., § 13.

Salsette is an island immediately to the north of Bombay, and is now included in the city limits. Bassein is a port immediately to the north of Salsette. Ever since the Mahrattas conquered the country from the Portuguese in 1739, Bombay was almost at their mercy. The East India Company was bent on acquiring Salsette and Bassein; whilst the Mahrattas were equally obstinate in refusing to part with either locality.

15. **Plots and Murders at Poona: Exile of Ragoba, 1774.**—The death of Mahdu Rao, Peishwa, was followed by plots and murders instigated by women. He had no son. Before he died he nominated his younger brother, Narain Rao, to succeed him as Peishwa; but he made friends with Ragoba, released him from prison, and appointed him regent and guardian. Once more there were bitter quarrels between an uncle and a nephew. Ragoba was imprisoned; Narain Rao was murdered. Ragoba became Peishwa and went away with an army to fight Hyder Ali of Mysore. In his absence the widow of Narain Rao gave birth to a son. Many believed that Ragoba was the murderer, egged on by his wife. Others believed that the infant was a fraud on the part of the widow. Ragoba however went into exile, and the infant became Peishwa under a Council of Regency.

16. **War with Poona: Stopped by Bengal, 1775-76.**—In this extremity Ragoba offered to cede Salsette and Bassein to Bombay if the British would help him to the throne at Poona. Bombay agreed to the terms and took possession of both places. Her army defeated the Council of Regency, and was about to conduct Ragoba to Poona, when the expedition was stopped from Bengal. Warren Hastings and his Council condemned the war, but ordered Bombay to keep possession of Salsette and Bassein.

17. **War with France: First Mahratta War, 1778-82.**—War, however, was inevitable. France was helping the United States of America in the struggle for independence. The Mahratta Council of Regency entertained a French envoy at Poona, and ceded the port of Chaul to France. The Council was divided between Sindhia and Holkar. The faction of Holkar invited Bombay to bring Ragoba to Poona; but when the Bombay expedition was approaching Poona, it was environed by the army of Sindhia, and surrendered to overwhelming numbers.

18. **Genius of Warren Hastings: Duel with Francis.**—Warren Hastings rose with the occasion. Death had removed one of his enemies in Council, and he could over-ride Philip Francis. He sent a force under Colonel Goddard through the heart of India to assail the Mahrattas in Guzerat. He sent another force under Captain Popham, to capture Sindhia's fortress at Gwalior. Philip Francis sent a challenge to Hastings, and was wounded in the duel and returned to England. In 1781-82 peace was concluded with the Mahrattas. Each side was bound over to give no help to the enemies of the other, and the British returned all their conquests to the Mahrattas excepting Salsette and Bassein.

19. **War with France: Hostilities of the Nizam and Hyder Ali, 1778-82.**—In 1778 the British began the war with France by the capture of Pondicherry. The Nizam was hostile but waited for events. Meanwhile Hyder Ali of Mysore was siding with France and the Mahrattas. Hyder Ali was a Mohammedan soldier who had risen to be commander-in-Chief of the army of the Hindu Raja of Mysore, and then had supplanted the Raja and usurped the sovereignty. In 1769 he had concluded an offensive and defensive alliance with the British at

Madras. Later on he was at war with the Mahrattas, and Madras could not help him because Bombay was expecting the friendly cession of Salsette and Bassein. Hyder Ali understood the clashing between Madras and Bombay, but professed to be offended and waited an opportunity for revenge.

20 **Hyder Ali invades the Carnatic, 1780-84: driven back by Sir Eyre Coote.**—Hyder Ali was bent on the conquest of Southern India. But for the Mahrattas of the Konkan and the British in the Carnatic he might have founded an empire as large as that of the old Maharajas of Vijayanagar. He conquered the Hindu Rajas on the Malabar side, but was unwilling to enter the Carnatic plain. At this crisis, the British captured the French settlement at Mahé on the western coast, which was under his protection. In his wrath he over-ran the Carnatic with 100,000 men, and spread terror and desolation up to the walls of Fort St. George. For a brief period he was sovereign of the Carnatic. Arcot and all the chief fortresses were in his possession. He appointed renters, collected the revenue and coined money. Fortunately Warren Hastings despatched an expedition under Sir Eyre Coote, which reached Madras in time to save the Company and the Nawab. Hyder Ali suffered several defeats and returned to his own territory. He died in 1782, and was succeeded by his son Tippu as Sultan of Mysore; and in 1784 a peace was concluded between Madras and Tippu.

21. **Parliamentary Interference: Board of Control, 1784.**—The wars in India were distasteful to the British nation, and seven commissioners were appointed by Parliament to serve as a Board of Control over the Court of Directors. Henceforth no war was to be declared, and no alliance to be formed with any Asiatic power, without the sanction of the Board of Control.

22. **Warren Hastings in England, 1785: Trial in Westminster Hall, 1788-94.**—Warren Hastings returned to England in 1785. By this time Philip Francis had poisoned the minds of Burke and Fox against him. He was impeached by the House of Commons and tried by the House of Lords in Westminster Hall. This trial is the centre of interest in Indian history. The main charges may be reduced to four heads, namely: unjust wars, corrupt receipt of money, demands on the Raja of Benares, and treatment of the Begums of Oudh.

23. (1) **Unjust Wars: Rohilla and Mahratta.**—Warren Hastings was responsible for the war against the Rohillas, but not for the wars against the Mahrattas. The Rohilla war was unjust because the British had no quarrel with the Rohillas. But Hastings and his Council were blinded by the half million offered to the East India Company. As regards the Mahratta war, Bombay began it; the Directors approved it; and Hastings did not promote it until the French appeared at Poona. The Mahrattas meant mischief. They could not possibly have sympathized with the American War of Independence. They encouraged France only because she was at war with England.

24. (2) **Corrupt Receipt of Money.**—The charges of corruption against Warren Hastings were never judicially proved. The same may be said of most charges of corruption in India, whether against Europeans or Asiatics. But Hastings never produced his accounts. Horace Walpole wrote at the time, "If Hastings is innocent, why does he give away so many diamonds?" After the lapse of a century nothing is to be gained by raking up such charges.

25. (3) **Demand on the Raja of Benares.**—Cheit Singh was a zemindar or renter of the district

of Benares, who had been raised to the rank of Raja. Warren Hastings, in accordance with the Moghul custom, called on him to pay a large contribution towards the expenses of the Mahratta war. Similar demands had been made on the British at Calcutta and Madras by the old Nawabs of Bengal and Carnatic. Cheit Singh refused to pay. A rebellion broke out at Benares, and Hastings had a narrow escape. Cheit Singh was deprived of his zemindari. Since then no demand has been made on Indian feudatories for a contribution towards war expenditure except by way of loan.

26. (4) **Treatment of the Oudh Begums.**—The charge of cruelty towards the Oudh Begums and their servants is much clearer. It was vehemently pressed in a brilliant speech by Sheridan, but when retold in simple language the eloquence loses force. The Nawab Vizier of Oudh died in 1775. He owed heavy sums to the East India Company. His mother and widow held large jaghirs, or resumable estates, for their support; and they also claimed the State treasures, estimated at two millions, as private property. In all this they were encouraged by two eunuchs, who managed their respective households, and kept much of the treasure in their own lodgings. Warren Hastings was of opinion that the British government ought not to interfere. But the British representative at Lucknow had guaranteed the money to the two Begums provided they paid a quarter of a million to the Company, and Philip Francis had induced the Council to sanction the arrangement. When Philip Francis had gone to England, the Bengal government was pressed for money for the Mahratta war. Hastings was assured that the Begums were implicated in the rebellion at Benares, in which he nearly lost his life. He withdrew the British guarantee, and encouraged the Nawab Vizier

to resume the jaghirs, and imprison the two eunuchs. In prison the eunuchs were tortured, and at last the treasures were surrendered. The Nawab Vizier paid off the debt to the Company, but the revenues of the jaghirs were restored to the Begums. The Nawab Vizier was responsible for the torture, but Hastings is not free from blame. He may have lost his temper; the Begums and their eunuchs may have driven him wild. He may have assumed that the Nawab Vizier would not proceed to extremities. But he could scarcely have expected that the Nawab Vizier would abstain from torture in enforcing a claim to treasure.

27. **Results of the Trial.**—Warren Hastings was acquitted, but not until the impeachment and trial had lasted more than seven years. That he was held in the highest esteem by the people of Bengal was testified by his successors, Lord Cornwallis and Sir John Shore. But the malice of Philip Francis was never idle, and has left to this day an indelible mark on the memory of Warren Hastings.

28. **Summary.**—The character and career of Warren Hastings are vexed questions to this day. His instincts were good, and his genius was undoubted, but his nature was warped by evil surroundings. He was not a born general like Clive, nor was he always a sound man of business like many of the old civilians; but he was the first Englishman in history who can be called an Indian statesman. He had none of the coarser vices of his time. He married the widow of a British officer in Bengal before he was twenty-four, and he lost her before he was twenty-seven. Ten years after her death, during his voyage to Madras, he fell in love with the wife of a portrait-painter named Imhoff, and afterwards married her, and this is the only weakness in his private

character. His systems of revenue and justice were not built upon the sand, like Lord Clive's dewani, but upon sure foundations, which have lasted till our own time. The war against the Mahrattas was marked by a daring strategy which alarmed the home authorities, but proved a brilliant success in India. Sir James Stephen observes, in his *History of Criminal Law*:—"The impeachment of Warren Hastings is, I think, a blot on the judicial history of the country. It was monstrous that a man should be tortured at irregular intervals for seven years in order that a singularly incompetent tribunal might be addressed before an excited audience by Burke and Sheridan, in language far removed from the calmness with which an advocate for the prosecution ought to address a criminal court." In 1813, in his eighty-first year, Warren Hastings was received with the utmost respect by the House of Commons when he tendered his evidence as regards the Company's charter. In 1814 he was raised to the Privy Council. But neither Pitt nor Grenville offered him a seat in the Cabinet, and he never entered the service of the Crown. He died in 1819 in his eighty-seventh year. His remains are buried in the church at Daylesford, his native place; and a bust and inscription in Westminster Abbey serve to perpetuate his memory.

CHAPTER IX.

RISE TO PARAMOUNT POWER, 1786–1828.

1. Lord Cornwallis, Governor-General, 1786–93.—2. War with Tippu: British alliance with Nizam: Vacillation of Mahrattas, 1790–92.—3. Idea of "Balance of Power": Mahrattas estranged.—4. Land Revenue: "Perpetual Settlement," 1793.—5. Omissions in the "Perpetual Settlement."—6. Sir John Shore, Governor-General, 1793–98: Non-intervention.—7. Sindhia's commanding position: supported by De Boigne.—8. Last Mahratta Coalition: Nizam overwhelmed, 1795.—9. Marquis of Wellesley, 1798–1805: downfall of Tippu, 1799.—10. Partition of Mysore.—11. Policy of Lord Wellesley: Maintenance of Peace by Subsidiary Alliances.—12. Nizam accepts Subsidiary Alliance.—13. Mahrattas reject.—14. Relative Strength: British and Mahratta, 1799–1802.—15. Rivalry between Sindhia and the Peishwa.—16. Rise of Jeswant Rao Holkar: Peishwa accepts Subsidiary Alliance.—17. Alarm of Sindhia and the Bhonslá, 1803: Victories of Wellesley and Lake.—18. Results of Lord Wellesley's Wars, 1803–05.—19. Suppression of Jeswant Rao Holkar.—20. Cornwallis, Barlow and Minto, 1805–13: Non-intervention.—21. Marquis of Hastings, 1813–23: War with Nipal, 1813–16.—22. Extermination of the Pindharies, 1817–18.—23. Extinction of the Peishwa of the Mahrattas.—24. Flight of the Raja of Nagpore.—25. Revolt of the Army of Holkar.—26. Peace in Rajputana.—27. Lord Amherst, 1823–28: Burma War, 1824–26.—28. Storming of Bhurtpore, 1826. 29. Summary.

1. **Lord Cornwallis, Governor-General, 1786-93.**—India and Europe were at peace. The three fighting powers of India—the Nizam, Tippu Sultan, and the Mahrattas—were watching each other. The

wars with France and America were over. Lord Cornwallis was sent to India as Governor-General and Commander-in-chief, with power to override his Council in case of necessity.

2. War with Tippu: British alliance with Nizam: Vacillation of Mahrattas, 1790-92.—Lord Cornwallis was expected to avoid war, but it was forced upon him. Tippu wantonly provoked the British government by attacking his Hindu neighbour, the Raja of Travancore, who had been brought under British protection. Lord Cornwallis prepared to take the field, and invited the Nizam and the Mahrattas to join in a war against Tippu, which would maintain the public peace in India. The Nizam accepted the alliance, as he wanted British protection against the Mahrattas, and Lord Cornwallis agreed to grant it until the end of the war. The Mahrattas shilly-shallied. They trimmed between the British and Tippu. They wanted an excuse for plundering Mysore, but they were offended at the British alliance with the Nizam. They promised to send a contingent to join the allies, whilst secretly offering to sell their services to Tippu and receiving his envoys at Poona. The war lasted over two years, and was brought to a close by the British advance on Seringapatam. Tippu was driven into a corner. He secured peace by ceding large territories, and paying a money contribution towards the expenses of the war.

3. Idea of "Balance of Power:" Mahrattas estranged.—The proposed alliances with the Nizam and the Mahrattas were approved by British statesmen as forming a basis for a balance of power, which neither party could violate without provoking the hostility of the other parties. But the scheme fell through. The Nizam could do nothing unless protected for the future against Mahratta demands.

The Mahrattas would do nothing unless permitted to collect chout from the Nizam, Tippu and other princes.

4. **Land Revenue: "Perpetual Settlement," 1793.**—Lord Cornwallis sought to reform the land revenue of Bengal by placing it on the English system of landed proprietors. He proclaimed a "Perpetual Settlement" in 1793, on the terms fixed in the latest leases. He turned the zemindars into proprietors with the power to dispose of their estates as they pleased, so long as the yearly assessment of the revenue was assured to the British government.

5. **Omissions in the "Perpetual Settlement."**—Two points were ignored in the "Perpetual Settlement." (1) The probable increase in the value of land, and extension of cultivation over areas of waste and jungle. (2) The possible rights of ryots with regard to possession or occupancy. It was indeed proposed at some future time to investigate such rights, but the design was never carried out.

6. **Sir John Shore, Governor-General, 1793-98: Non-intervention.**—Sir John Shore was a Bengal civilian who was expected to walk in the ways of Lord Cornwallis. He could not protect the Nizam against the Mahrattas without violating the policy of non-intervention laid down by the Home authorities. The result was that the Nizam tried to protect himself by employing M. Raymond, a Frenchman, to raise and drill an army of sepoy battalions under the command of European officers.

7. **Sindhia's commanding position: supported by De Boigne.**—Meanwhile Mahadaji Sindhia had grown more powerful than ever. During the war against Tippu, he engaged De Boigne, a gentleman from Savoy, to create an army on the European system. De Boigne enlisted Afghans and Hindu-

stanis as well as Mahrattas, and organised them in battalions, drilled, disciplined, and commanded, as far as possible, by Europeans. To these was added a formidable train of artillery. With this force Sindhia might have become paramount in the Deccan as well as in Hindustan. He died in 1794, and was succeeded by Daulat Rao Sindhia, a boy of fourteen.

8. **Last Mahratta Coalition: Nizam overwhelmed, 1795.**—The Mahrattas presumed on British non-intervention to unite in vast demands on the Nizam. For the last time in India the Peishwa was supported by all his lieutenants, by Sindhia and Holkar as well as by the Gaekwar and the Bhonslá. The Nizam was utterly crushed in the battle of Kurdla. Later on the first Napoleon was making a descent on Egypt in the hope of reaching India, and Lord Mornington, better known by his later title of the Marquis of Wellesley, was appointed Governor-General of Bengal.

9. **Marquis of Wellesley, 1798-1805: downfall of Tippu, 1799.**—Scarcely had the new Governor-General landed at Calcutta, when it was known that Tippu had concluded an offensive and defensive alliance with the French at Mauritius. Such an alliance was a menace to the British empire. France was threatening Great Britain and Napoleon was proposing to invade India. The extinction of Tippu was an imperial necessity, and war was inevitable. Lord Wellesley sought to revive the alliances with the Nizam and the Mahrattas against Tippu, but demanded the disbandment of the French battalions. The Nizam accepted the alliance and the Frenchmen left his service. The Mahrattas, however, held aloof. The young Peishwa was dead, and Baji Rao, a son of Ragoba, had succeeded to the throne at Poona. Neither the new Peishwa nor his lieutenants would

abandon their demands for chout against the Nizam. Daulat Rao Sindhia was inclined to support Tippu against the British, and refused to sacrifice his French battalions. Tippu, however, was doomed. One British army advanced from Madras and another from Bombay. Seringapatam was taken by storm and Tippu was found dead in the gateway.

10. **Partition of Mysore.**—The Mohammedan dominion of Hyder Ali was broken up. The kingdom of Mysore, which he had wrested from the Hindu Raja forty years before, was restored to a boy representative of the family. The outlying territories were divided into three shares, one was taken by Lord Wellesley for the East India Company ; a second was given to the Nizam; the third was offered to the Mahrattas.

11. **Policy of Lord Wellesley: Maintenance of Peace by Subsidiary Alliances.**—Lord Wellesley was determined that the British government should become the paramount power in India. No other power could keep the peace and resist French invasion. No other power could protect India from the Mahrattas, or curb the religious animosities and antagonisms of ages. In a word, Lord Wellesley proposed to govern India by a scheme which was a novelty in history. Every state was to cede sufficient territory for the maintenance of a standing army, which was to be at the disposal of the paramount power for putting down all wars and feuds, all revolts or revolutions of every sort and kind.

12. **Nizam accepts Subsidiary Alliance.**—The Nizam accepted Lord Wellesley's conditions. He was protected from the Mahrattas, but he was bound over by treaty not to make war, or negotiate with any prince or potentate whatever, or entertain any Europeans in his service, without the consent of

the British government. A sepoy army commanded by British officers was raised in the room of the disbanded French battalions. It was known as the "Hyderabad Subsidiary Force." It was paid out of the revenues of the Nizam's shares of Mysore territory. It was under the orders of the British government, and could be employed against any enemy of the public peace, within or without the Nizam's territory.

13. **Mahrattas reject.**—Lord Wellesley offered the third Mysore share to the Mahrattas provided they would agree to similar terms. The Peishwa shilly-shallied. He would receive the share in satisfaction of Mahratta claims to chout in Mysore. He would accept a "Poona Subsidiary Force" of sepoys commanded by British officers, provided he might employ it against Sindhia, Holkar or other refractory lieutenants, as well as in the collection of chout. But neither the Peishwa nor Sindhia would dismiss the Frenchmen in their service or accept the British government as the arbiter of peace and war.

14. **Relative Strength: British and Mahratta, 1799-1802.**—The main stumbling-block to peace was the Mahratta chout. The Mahrattas seemed to claim a divine right to chout. The area of chout, however, was closing in. The Nawab of the Carnatic had been deposed for intriguing with the enemies of the British government, and the Carnatic was added to the Madras Presidency. The Nawab Vizier of Oudh had ceded territories in discharge of his debt to the East India Company, and the British frontier was pushed westward to Cawnpore. Consequently Bengal, Oudh, the Nizam's Deccan, Madras and Mysore were barred against the Mahrattas by a British cordon. Most of the territories now occupied by the North-West Provinces were however at their mercy; so was Guzerat, Raj-

putana, Malwa, Bundelkund, and the present Bombay Presidency. From the Ganges on the north to the Nerbudda on the south, and from the Nerbudda still futher south to the Kistna, the Mahrattas were the domineering and destroying power.

15. **Rivalry between Sindhia and the Peishwa.**—Meanwhile the Mahratta confederacy was breaking up. The Peishwa and Sindhia were both young men, plotting against each other under a mask of friendship, the Brahman against the warrior. Daulat Rao Sindhia was the rising man. The Peishwa was weak, and had no one but Sindhia to protect him against his lieutenants. De Boigne had left India warning Sindhia not to offend the British, and advising him to disband his battalions rather than provoke a war. But Sindhia was stubborn. Perron, the successor of De Boigne, hated the British. Sindhia was puffed up with arrogance. He was master of the Padishah at Delhi, and would have been master of the Peishwa at Poona, when he was called away to Indore by the death of Holkar.

16. **Rise of Jeswant Rao Holkar: Peishwa accepts Subsidiary Alliance.**—At Indore Sindhia was checkmated by an illegitimate prince of the house of Holkar, a rebel outlaw of the stamp of Sivaji. Jeswant Rao Holkar suddenly appeared with an army of freebooting horsemen. He was routed by Sindhia's French battalions, but moved off to Poona, and defeated the army of the young Peishwa—Baji Rao. His victory spread a wild alarm. The Peishwa fled to the coast and escaped by sea to Bassein; and then accepted the subsidiary alliance offered by Lord Wellesley on condition of being restored by the British to his throne at Poona.

17. **Alarm of Sindhia and the Bhonslá, 1803: Victories of Wellesley and Lake.**—

The Mahratta lieutenants were bewildered by the surrender of the Peishwa. Their sovereign was restored to the kingdom of the Konkan without his sovereignty. The Peishwa was no longer the supreme head of the Mahratta confederacy, but a vassal of the British government. The Gaekwar of Baroda followed the example of the Peishwa, and accepted the subsidiary alliance. Sindhia and the Bhonslá Raja of Berar were sorely perplexed. They were at the head of large armies in the Deccan; whilst the Holkar outlaw returned to Indore, seized the kingdom, and declined to join in any attack on the British. By the end of 1803 the war was begun and over. Sindhia and the Bhonslá in the Deccan were utterly defeated by Colonel Arthur Wellesley at Assaye and Argaum. The French battalions of Sindhia in Hindustan were defeated by General Lake at Alighur and Laswari; Delhi and Agra were captured by the British; and the old Padishah, Shah Alam, was once more taken under British protection.

18. **Results of Lord Wellesley's Wars, 1803-05.**—The British government was master of India. The supremacy of Sindhia had vanished for ever. He lost his footing at Delhi, and abandoned all territories to the northward of the Jumna. The Bhonslá surrendered Berar and Orissa, and was henceforth known as the Raja of Nagpore. The princes and chiefs of Rajputana were taken under British protection. The public peace was kept by subsidiary armies. Berar was added to the territory of the Nizam. Orissa, on the Bay of Bengal, was kept by the British government because it commanded the sea. The seaboard of India was British territory from Guzerat to Bengal.

19. **Suppression of Jeswant Rao Holkar.**—But Jeswant Rao Holkar of Indore was still uncon-

quered. He set the British government at defiance by collecting plunder and chout in Rajputana. General Lake drove him back to his own territories in Malwa, but he returned during the rains, repulsed a British detachment under Colonel Monson, and was supported by Sindhia and the Rajputs. After giving considerable trouble he was forced to surrender. Sindhia repented and rejoined the British alliance, and Jeswant Rao Holkar died a few years afterwards at Indore.

20. **Cornwallis, Barlow and Minto, 1805-13: Non-Intervention.**—The British nation was alarmed at the uprising of Holkar. It did not appreciate the victories of Lord Wellesley, or believe in the future peace of India. Lord Cornwallis was sent out to conciliate the Mahratta princes, but died shortly afterwards. Sir George Barlow, a Bengal civilian, was Governor-General until 1807, and was then succeeded by Lord Minto. Great Britain was engaged in the struggle against France and Napoleon, and Rajputana was abandoned to Mahrattas and Afghans. Brigand leaders founded principalities, and assumed the rank of Rajas and Nawabs. Hosts of marauders, under the name of Pindharies, burrowed during the rains in the wilds of Malwa, and then broke out in the dry season, and plundered and desolated the villages far and wide. Rajputana was exhausted, and at last the Pindharies began to violate the territories of the British government and its allies.

21. **Marquis of Hastings, 1813-23: War with Nipal, 1813-16.**—Lord Moira, better known as the Marquis of Hastings, was forced to leave the Pindharies alone for awhile. The Ghorkas, who had conquered Nipal on the Himalayas some fifty years before, were beginning to menace British India from

the northward. They were annexing British villages along the frontier, and threatening to extend their dominion to the Ganges. Lord Hastings was forced to declare war. British armies ascended the Himalayas to the neighbourhood of Katmandu, the capital of Nipal, and captured fortresses which the Ghorkas deemed impregnable. Peace was concluded in 1816, but no subsidiary army was required from Nipal.

22. **Extermination of the Pindharies, 1817-18.**—Lord Hastings next prepared to exterminate the Pindharies. A Bengal army from the north and a Madras army from the south began to environ their camps in Malwa. Many were slain or perished in the jungle; but many surrendered, and settled down as peaceful cultivators. Within a few months the Pindhari gangs, which for generations had been the pest of Hindustan and the Deccan, disappeared for ever from India.

23. **Extinction of the Peishwa of the Mahrattas.**—Baji Rao, Peishwa of the Mahrattas, had never been reconciled to the loss of sovereignty. He had been delivered from the thraldom of Sindhia. He had been restored to the throne at Poona after his flight from Holkar. But the days of chout were over, and he was no longer the suzerain of predatory princes. He grew restless and mischievous. He was implicated in the murder of an envoy from the Gaekwar of Baroda, who had been permitted to visit Poona. He was secretly stirring up the Mahratta princes to revolt. Whilst the Poona Subsidiary Force was engaged in suppressing the Pindharies, he attacked a British detachment at Khirki near Poona, and was beaten back in spite of his overwhelming numbers. When the Subsidiary Force had returned to Poona, Baji Rao took flight and fled into the jungle. After a few months he was environed by

British troops, and surrendered to save his life. His kingdom was added to the Bombay Presidency, and he passed the remainder of his days as a British pensioner at Bithoor near Cawnpore.

24. **Flight of the Raja of Nagpore.**—Meanwhile the Raja of Nagpore suddenly declared for the Peishwa, and attacked the British Residency. The battle was fought on Sitabuldi hill, between the city of Nagpore and the Residency. It will always be famous in the annals of India. The Raja relied on a strong force of Arab mercenaries, but they were beaten back by Bengal cavalry. The Raja fled from Nagpore and forfeited his kingdom; but Lord Hastings ordered an infant nephew to be placed upon the throne as his successor.

25. **Revolt of the Army of Holkar.**—At this time the reigning Holkar was an infant, and the army was bought over by Baji Rao, and declared for the Peishwa. The army, however, was routed by the British in the battle of Mehidpore. The infant Holkar was restored to his throne, and a Subsidiary Force was maintained at Indore.

26. **Peace in Rajputana.**—The princes and chiefs in Rajputana were henceforth protected from the Mahrattas. They were bound over to keep the peace and accept the British government as the arbiter of all disputes. Thus for the first time in recorded history peace was established from the Himalayas to Comorin, from the banks of the Sutlej to the mouths of the Ganges.

27. **Lord Amherst, 1823-28: Burma War, 1824-26.**—Lord Amherst expected to rule India in peace, but the Burmese forced on a war. They invaded British territory and threatened to conquer Bengal and carry off the Governor-General in golden

fetters. A British expedition was sent to Rangoon, and eventually the king of Ava sued for peace. Arakan and Tenasserim became British territory, and so did Cachar and Assam to the eastward of Bengal.

28. **Storming of Bhurtpore, 1826.**—In 1825 the principality of Bhurtpore set the British government at defiance. An infant Raja had been recognised by the British government, and placed on the throne under the guardianship of an uncle. The uncle was murdered by a rebel kinsman who defied the British government, and secured himself in the huge mud fortress of Bhurtpore. In 1826 a British force mined the walls and took the fortress by storm. The usurper was carried away as a state prisoner, and the infant Raja was restored. Henceforth the British government was accepted by the princes and people of India as paramount and sovereign.

29. **Summary.**—An interval of forty years separates Lord Amherst from Warren Hastings. Within a single generation Bengal had grown from a province or principality into an Anglo-Indian empire. Three distinct lines of policy had been tried in turns by the British government. 1st. Lord Cornwallis sought to realise the European idea of a balance of power. 2nd. Sir John Shore reverted to the old idea of the East India Company of isolation and non-intervention. 3rd. Lord Wellesley tried the imperial experiment of keeping the peace of India by asserting the paramount power. This plan would have succeeded at once but for the outbreak of Jeswant Rao Holkar. It remained in abeyance under Sir George Barlow and Lord Minto. It was forced on Lord Hastings by the raids of the Pindharies and revolt of the Peishwa, and on Lord Amherst by the aggressions of the king of Burma and the revolt at Bhurtpore.

CHAPTER X.

PEACE AND PROGRESS: BENTINCK AND METCALFE, 1828-36.

1. **Lord William Bentinck, 1828-35.**—The administration of Lord William Bentinck was an era of peace and progress. The old wars were over. Conquered territories were settling down under British rule. The spirit of reform which was rampant in the British Isles was breathing a new life into Anglo-Indian statesmen.

2. **Abolition of Suttees and Thugs.**—Lord William Bentinck abolished Suttees (properly, Satís), or the burning of living widows with their dead husbands; a hideous rite which had been practised by Hindus from the remotest antiquity. He sanctioned an agency for the suppression of Thugs, or gangs of hereditary garroters, who strangled travel-

lers unawares, and then rifled and buried them within a few moments, without leaving a trace behind. Two generations have scarcely passed away, and Satís and Thugs have almost ceased to be.

3. **Moral and Material Progress.**—Lord William Bentinck was the first Governor-General who sought to advance the masses. He promoted English education in the room of Oriental learning. He launched steamers on the Ganges to ply between Calcutta and Allahabad, and laboured to open the Overland Route to Europe. He encouraged social intercourse between Europeans and Asiatics, and set the example in his entertainments at Government House. He declared that neither race, religion, nor colour should be a disqualification for the public service; and he enforced the rule by appointing Asiatics to be deputy-collectors and subordinate civil judges.

4. **Revenue Survey and Settlement, 1832.**—Lord William Bentinck ordered a Survey of village areas, and a Settlement of the land revenue in the North-West Provinces. Every village area was to be mapped, and every field within it to be measured and valued. All boundaries were to be marked out by British officers, with the help of native punchayets, or local village arbitrators. In like manner, all rights in the land were to be duly investigated, whether of zemindars, who are here known as talukdars, or of joint village proprietors, or of under-proprietors, who are known as village zemindars, or of ryots old and new. The result was that family holdings, co-shares, revenues, rents, and all other necessary details, of fifty millions of acres of village lands in the North-West Provinces were entered in the village books with scrupulous accuracy, and preserved for all future time.

5. Village Records: Maps and Registers.—The history of the "Surveys and Settlements" which followed would fill a library. They have been carried out in every presidency and province in India excepting Bengal. They have been enlarged by minute classifications of the soils. In the present day the maps and registers of village areas in India are as perfect as the plans and rent-rolls of private estates in the British Isles.

6. Hindu Village System: Brotherhoods of Joint Proprietors.—The village community comprises all the elements of a Hindu body politic. A clan or brotherhood of colonists settled down like a swarm of bees and covered a village area. Sometimes they became the owners by the right of conquest, and compelled the previous villagers to labour as serfs or slaves. Sometimes they cleared an area of virgin land in the uncultured waste, and became owners by the right of first occupation. They formed a little republic or commonwealth, of which they, the village aristocracy, were the rulers. They let out lands they did not want to outsiders or later arrivals, and shared the rents or crops. They were jointly responsible for the payment of a yearly revenue to the sovereign power for the time being. They had their own head man, village accountant, and village watchman or constable, who may have been originally elected by the brotherhood, but who gradually became hereditary.

7. Tenants and Artisans.—Below the village aristocracy of landholders was a village population of tenants, traders, professionals, such as priest, schoolmaster, medicine man, and money lender; and the usual ruck of artisans and labourers. These were all distributed into castes, and every caste had its own head man, and its own laws and customs. Every caste was hereditary.

8. **Zemindars of Bengal.**—The Moghuls conquered Bengal, but they never liked the climate. They never settled down on the lands in Bengal as they did on those in the North-West Provinces. They left the collection of the revenue to zemindars, who were often foreigners from Persia, caring nothing for hereditary rights, and only anxious to make money. Village systems were broken up, village proprietors disappeared, village officials became the servants of the zemindar, and village cultivators became tenants at will.

9. **Village Proprietors in the North-West Provinces.**—The North-West Provinces, on the other hand, were the home of the Moghuls in India; their empire proper, with the two time-honoured capitals at Delhi and Agra. Village communities were better preserved. Joint village proprietors cultivated the lands from father to son, which had been held by the old brotherhoods or clans from time immemorial. But when the Moghul empire was breaking up, and Afghans and Mahrattas were fighting for the mastery, the village communities became the prey of military adventurers of all kinds, who acquired large estates by force of arms, or by dubious grants from the puppet Padishah, and exacted rents from villages regardless of all rights of proprietorship or prescription. Many were driven to migrate elsewhere, but they never forgot the old village or its landmarks; and after the lapse of a generation or two, the old families often returned and re-occupied the old sites with the instinctive love of home; and the squatters who had cultivated the land in their absence, were compelled by the sheer force of public opinion to surrender it. Accordingly the result of the "Survey and Settlement" was that some of the later interlopers lost their estates, whilst the bulk of the old joint proprietors recovered their ancestral villages.

10. **Ryots in the Madras and Bombay Presidencies.**—Joint village proprietors had disappeared from the Madras and Bombay Presidencies. Village communities, however, remained with their hereditary head men and officials, ryots, professionals, and artisans. Accordingly the bulk of the land revenue was settled with individual ryots. Surveys and Settlements of recent date have reduced rents. Reduced rentals have enlarged the area of cultivation, enhanced the value of individual holdings, and led to a large increase in the aggregate revenue from the land.

11. **East India Company Retires from Business, 1813-33.**—Under Lord William Bentinck the East India Company ceased to be traders. They had held the monopoly from the days of Queen Elizabeth. In 1813 the trade with India had been thrown open to all British subjects. In 1833 the trade with China was thrown open, and the East India Company was restricted to the work of administration. Europeans who had hitherto been prohibited from dwelling in India without a license, were permitted to reside wherever they pleased. In India the commercial branch of the civil service was abolished, and nothing remained but the three administrative departments of revenue, judicial, and political. The charter of the Company was renewed for twenty years, and in 1853 was to be again brought under consideration.

12. **Government of India: Legislative Council.**—The Governor-General in Council was henceforth known as the Government of India, and controlled Madras and Bombay, as well as a fourth Presidency known as the North-West Provinces. No Presidency could spend extra money without its authority. No Presidency could make laws, but all law making was reserved for the Governor-General

and his Council sitting at Calcutta. A new law member was appointed from England to draft bills, and especially to draft a new Penal Code, but otherwise the new Legislative Council was essentially Bengal. Mr., afterwards Lord Macaulay, was the first law member, but without a seat in the Executive Council.

13. **Sir Charles Metcalfe, Provisional Governor-General; Liberty of the Press, 1835-36.**—Lord William Bentinck returned to England in 1835, and Sir Charles Metcalfe, a Bengal civilian, was provisional Governor-General. Sir Charles Metcalfe believed that the future of India depended on the extension of British influence. He gave liberty to the press in India, and Macaulay drafted the bill. The Court of Directors was grievously offended. Sir Charles Metcalfe retired from the service of the East India Company, and entered that of the Crown. Eventually he was created Lord Metcalfe.

14. **Summary.**—The administrations of Lord William Bentinck and Sir Charles Metcalfe begin a new era in the history of India. The Indian wars of their predecessors established the reign of peace. The advance of their successors into Central Asia was undertaken to guard India against foreign invasion. The interval was marked by four important measures. First, the organization of a systematic survey and settlement of the land. Second, the prohibition of the East India Company and its servants from all concern in trade. Third, the opening out of India to European settlers. Fourth, the centralization of all legislation in India in the Governor-General and Council at Calcutta, with the addition of a law member from England who was excluded from all share in the executive.

CHAPTER XI.

CENTRAL ASIA: PUNJAB, SIND, AFGHANISTAN, 1836–53.

1. North-West Frontier: River Sutlej and Sind Valley.—2. Central Asia, 1600–1800: Punjab, Sind, and Afghanistan.—3. Threatened Advance of Napoleon, 1800–1810.—4. Russian Advance: Three barriers of Bokhara, Afghanistan and the Punjab, 1830-36.—5. Rise of Dost Mohammed Khan: Flight of Shah Shuja into British territory.—6. Trade up the River Indus.—7. LORD AUCKLAND, 1836–42: Persian Siege of Herat, 1837.—8. First Kábul War, 1838: Restoration of Shah Shuja, 1839–40.—9. British Disasters in Kábul, 1841–42: Murder of Burnes and Macnaghten.—10. LORD ELLENBOROUGH, 1842–44: Avenging Army under Pollock.—11. Conquest of Sind, 1843.—12. Revolt of Sindhia's Army; War in Gwalior, 1843.—13. Anarchy in the Punjab: Recall of Lord Ellenborough, 1844.—14. LORD HARDINGE, 1844–48.—15. First Sikh War: Campaign on the Sutlej, 1845–46.—16. Sikh Government under British Protection, 1846–48.—17. LORD DALHOUSIE, 1848–56: Revolt at Multan.—18. Sikh Insurrection, 1848.—19. Second Sikh War: British Conquest of the Punjab, 1848–49.—20. Board and Chief Commissioner: Lord Dalhousie, Governor.—21. Final Relations with Dost Mohammed Khan of Afghanistan, 1849–57.—22. Summary.

1. **North-West Frontier: River Sutlej and Sind Valley.**—The river Sutlej, which flows into the upper Indus, and the Sind valley on the lower Indus, were the limits of the British empire on the north-west. The Punjab, or "land of five rivers," westward of the Sutlej, was governed by Runjeet Singh, a famous Sikh warrior, who was called the "Lion of Lahore." The Sind valley was governed

by four Mohammedan kinsmen who were known as the Amirs of Sind. Still further westward was Afghanistan, with its four divisions of Kábul (or Caubool), Kandahar, Herat, and Afghan Turkistan.

2. **Central Asia, 1600–1800: Punjab, Sind, and Afghanistan.**—All these territories, with Kashmir and others, were conquered by Akbar, the founder of the Moghul empire. During the seventeenth century they were known to European travellers. Tavernier, the French jeweller, travelled from Persia to India *viâ* Kandahar. Bernier, the French physician, accompanied the camp of Aurangzeb from Delhi to Kashmir *viâ* Lahore. During the first quarter of the eighteenth century the Afghans invaded Persia. Later on the Persians, under Nadir Shah, invaded India. During the latter half of the same century, the whole of Central Asia was included in the Afghan empire founded by Ahmed Shah Abdali. After the death of Ahmed Shah, in 1773, the region was hidden from Europe by wars between his sons, and Central Asia was as little known as Central Africa.

3. **Threatened Advance of Napoleon, 1800–1810.**—In the early years of the nineteenth century India was threatened by Napoleon Buonaparte. That restless warrior proposed to follow the footsteps of Alexander; to conquer Persia, advance through Central Asia and invade India. British envoys were sent to Persia and Afghanistan to form defensive alliances with those powers; but meanwhile Europe was armed against the common enemy, and the panic died out in Asia.

4. **Russian Advance: Three barriers of Bokhara, Afghanistan and the Punjab, 1830–36.**—In the days of Lord William Bentinck there were rumours of Russian movements in the same direction. Three successive barriers separated Russia

from India proper, or Hindustan. First, BOKHARA, including the three Usbeg Khanates of Khiva, Bokhara, and Khokand. Second, AFGHANISTAN, including Kábul, Kandahar, Herat, and Afghan Turkistan. Third, PUNJAB, under Runjeet Singh, the "Lion of Lahore." Runjeet was our nearest neighbour. The British did not interfere with his conquests so long as he kept to his own side of the Sutlej, and did not attack the Amirs of Sind. On the north he conquered the mountain region which included Kashmir. On the west he wrested the valley of Peshawar from the Afghans. The loss of Peshawar was bitterly felt. It was the high road from the Khyber Pass to the Attock Fort, by which the Afghans had entered the Punjab from the earliest days of Mohammedan invasion.

5. **Rise of Dost Mohammed Khan: Flight of Shah Shuja into British territory.**—Meanwhile, amidst a confusion of jars and wars, the ruling power in Afghanistan was transferred from the sovereign to the minister. Dost Mohammed Khan, the Barukzai, became Amir, whilst Shah Shuja, the Durani, fled into British territory and found refuge as a political exile.

6. **Trade up the River Indus.**—Schemes were afloat for opening out a trade with Central Asia up the river Indus. The Afghans had nothing to do with the Indus. They were shut out from the river by the valley of Peshawar and mountain range of Soliman. The upper course was commanded by Runjeet Singh, and the lower course by the Amirs of Sind. Neither Runjeet Singh nor the Amirs of Sind were alive to the advantages of trade. Runjeet Singh professed the warmest friendship for the British government, but he refused to admit British traders into his dominions. The Amirs of Sind were equally exclusive, but were induced against their will to permit the British to navigate the Indus.

7. **Lord Auckland, 1836–42: Persian Siege of Herat, 1837.**—In 1837 Persia laid siege to Herat, and was supposed to do so in the interest of Russia. Dost Mohammed Khan was sorely tried. The British would have helped the Afghans to keep Herat, but the Dost wanted Lord Auckland to induce Runjeet Singh to restore the valley of Peshawar. Lord Auckland would not interfere about Peshawar, as it would have given mortal offence to Runjeet Singh. Dost Mohammed was offended in his turn, and received a Russian envoy at Kábul. Accordingly Lord Auckland resolved to oust him from the throne at Kábul and restore Shah Shuja the exile.

8. **First Kâbul War, 1838: Restoration of Shah Shuja, 1839–40.**—Persia retired from Herat, but meantime the British army took the field. It would not anger Runjeet Singh by marching through the Punjab, but crossed the Indus in Sind territory. A small British force was left at Kandahar under General Nott and Major Rawlinson. The main army, under Sir John Keane, stormed the fortress of Ghazni, and then advanced to Kábul. Shah Shuja was enthroned at Kábul, but Sir William Macnaghten was British Resident and guardian. Dost Mohammed Khan fled northward over the Oxus into Bokhara, but returned in 1840 and surrendered himself as prisoner to Macnaghten. He was conducted to Calcutta, and kindly treated by the British government.

9. **British Disasters in Kabul, 1841–42: Murder of Burnes and Macnaghten.**—Runjeet Singh died at Lahore in 1839. His successor was anxious for British support, and permitted British troops to march through the Punjab. Sir John, now Lord Keane, returned to India, and was succeeded by General Elphinstone at Kábul. Meanwhile the Afghans, and especially the Hill tribes between

Kábul and the Punjab, had grown disaffected. Large subsidies had been paid to them for several months, and then stopped. In 1841 there was an outbreak at Kábul fomented by Akbar Khan, the eldest son of Dost Mohammed. Sir Alexander Burnes, who was about to succeed Macnaghten as British Resident, was murdered in the city. Macnaghten opened up negotiations with Akbar Khan for a return to the Punjab, but was murdered at the meeting. The British army began to retreat towards the Khyber Pass,[1] but was pursued by a large army of Afghans under Akbar Khan. The snow began to fall and the heights on either side were crowded by Hill tribes who poured down a deadly fire. The retreating force perished in the snow or was killed by the musketry, and only one man escaped to tell the story.

10. **Lord Ellenborough, 1842-44: Avenging Army under Pollock.**—General Nott and Major Rawlinson were still at Kandahar. In 1842 an avenging army marched through the Punjab under General Pollock, drove the Hill tribes from the heights above the Khyber Pass, and advanced to Kábul, where it was joined by the force from Kandahar. Shah Shuja was dead and Dost Mohammed was restored to his throne at Kábul.

11. **Conquest of Sind, 1843.**—The Sind Amirs were encouraged by British disasters to violate their treaty engagements with the British government. Other States were inclined to follow the bad example, but Lord Ellenborough stopped the disaffection by declaring war against Sind. The Amirs were defeated at Miani and Hyderabad on the Indus, and the Sind valley was added to the Bombay Presidency.

[1] The scene of this catastrophe has sometimes been laid in the "Khyber Pass;" properly speaking it lay in the "Kurd Kabul" and "Jugduluk" Passes, which lead from the city of Kábul to the Khyber.

12. **Revolt of Sindhia's Army: War in Gwalior, 1843.**—Meanwhile the army of Sindhia had become costly and dangerous. It consumed two-thirds of the revenues of Gwalior, and domineered over the Mahratta government. The last Sindhia had died leaving no son natural or adopted. His widow, a girl of twelve, adopted a boy of eight, and acted as regent at Gwalior during his minority. She bought over the army by largesses, and set the British government at defiance. Lord Ellenborough entered Gwalior territory with a British force. Sindhia's army was defeated at Maharajpore and Punniar. The girl widow was removed from power and pensioned off. A Council of Regency was set up in her room, and a subsidiary force was raised under the command of British officers, which was known as the Gwalior Contingent.

13. **Anarchy in the Punjab: Recall of Lord Ellenborough, 1844.**—Ever since the death of Runjeet Singh in 1839, the Punjab had been sinking into anarchy. Plots amongst ministers and nobles, outbreaks in the court and camp, assassinations and vicious indulgences in high places, removed princes and generals with appalling rapidity. The Sikh army, which submitted to the iron will of Runjeet Singh, seemed to have broken loose under his degenerate successors. It was a religious commonwealth, split up into little committees, or punchayets, of common soldiers known as Khalsas, or "saved ones," who gave the law to the officers. The "army of the Khalsa," as it was called, was made up of fiery zealots, equally ready to sack and kill in the name of God and the Sikh Guru. Lord Ellenborough foresaw that the Sikhs would sooner or later cross the Sutlej for the invasion of Hindustan. Indeed this was one reason why he broke up the army of Sindhia, and prevented any possible coalition

between Sikhs and Mahrattas. At this juncture he was recalled.

14. **Lord Hardinge, 1844-48.**—Sir Henry, afterwards Lord Hardinge, succeeded Lord Ellenborough in July, 1844. The Punjab was boiling over with turmoil. The British government watched the convulsions with anxiety, and was suddenly aroused by the Sikh invasion of Hindustan.

15. **First Sikh War: Campaign on the Sutlej, 1845-46.**—The child Dhuleep Singh, a reputed son of old Runjeet Singh, was placed on the throne in 1843 by the Sikh army. The queen mother was regent, her paramour was minister, and a reckless schemer was commander-in-chief. All three were in mortal fear of the soldiers of the Khalsa. The Sikh army was preparing to storm and sack the city of Lahore, when it was ordered to invade British territory. The British government was taken by surprise. The Sikh army crossed the Sutlej in December, 1845, and advanced to Moodki. Then followed the victories of Moodki and Ferozeshahar and the Sikh retreat to the Punjab. In January, 1846, the Sikhs recrossed the Sutlej into British territory. By this time the British artillery was brought up from Delhi. The Sikhs were defeated at Aliwal. Then followed the crowning victory of Lord Hardinge and Lord Gough at Sobraon, and the advance of the British army to Lahore.

16. **Sikh Government under British Protection, 1846-48.**—Lord Hardinge entrusted the government of the Punjab to a Council of Regency, consisting of Sikh nobles under the guidance of Sir Henry Lawrence as British Resident. He refused to create a subsidiary army, but he left a British force to protect the government until the boy Dhuleep Singh reached his majority. Two-thirds of the Sikh

army of the Khalsa were disbanded. The Jullunder Doab between the Sutlej and the Beyas was added to the British empire. The mountain territories on the north, which included Kashmir, were ceded to the local chief, Golab Singh, on payment of a million sterling, and acknowledgment of British supremacy.

17. **Lord Dalhousie, 1848-56: Revolt at Multan.**—Lord Dalhousie succeeded Lord Hardinge in 1848. Shortly afterwards the Punjab was again in commotion. Sikh government under British protection had failed to keep the peace. The army of the Khalsa had disappeared, but the old love of license and plunder was burning in the hearts of the disbanded soldiery. The Sikh governor of Multan revolted; two Englishmen were murdered. A British force besieged the rebels in Multan. It was joined by a Sikh force in the service of the Council of Regency commanded by Shere Singh.

18. **Sikh Insurrection, 1848.**—So far the revolt at Multan was regarded as a single outbreak which would be soon suppressed by the capture of the fortress. In reality it was the beginning of a general insurrection. Shere Singh, who commanded the Sikh force in the besieging army, suddenly deserted the British force and joined his father Chutter Singh, who was already in open rebellion. The revolt was secretly promoted by the queen mother, and spread over the Punjab like wildfire. The old soldiers of the Khalsa rallied round Shere Singh and his father. The half-and-half government set up by Lord Hardinge was unable to cope with a revolution which was restoring the old anarchy.

19. **Second Sikh War: British Conquest of the Punjab, 1848-49.**—In November, 1848, Lord Gough advanced against the rebel army. Then fol-

lowed the famous campaign between the Chenab and Jhelum rivers about 100 miles to the north of Lahore. In January, 1849, Lord Gough fought the dubious battle of Chillianwallah, near the spot where Alexander the Great crossed the Jhelum and defeated the army of Porus. Meanwhile Multan surrendered, and the besieging force joined Lord Gough. In February the Sikh army was utterly defeated at Gujerat. The conquest of the Punjab was complete. All previous treaties and engagements with the Sikhs were rendered null and void by the revolt. Lord Dalhousie annexed the Punjab, and formed it into a separate province of the British empire. A provision, however, of five lakhs of rupees per annum, or fifty thousand pounds sterling, was made for Dhuleep Singh and other members of the family of Runjeet Singh out of the revenues of the conquered territory.

20. **Board and Chief Commissioner: Lord Dalhousie, Governor.**—Lord Dalhousie placed the Punjab under a Board, and then under a Chief Commissioner. He thus kept the government of the new province in his own hands. He appointed every officer in the administration, regulated all promotions, and supervised all proceedings. In the older provinces such details were left to the discretion of a Governor in Council or a Lieutenant-Governor; but Lord Dalhousie was bent on controlling the administration of the Punjab until British rule was developed enough to warrant the appointment of a Lieutenant-Governor.

21. **Final Relations with Dost Mohammed Khan of Afghanistan, 1849-57.**—At the outbreak of the rebellion, the Sikh leaders had ceded the long coveted valley of Peshawar to Dost Mohammed Khan on condition that he helped them against the British. The Dost accepted the terms so far as to occupy the

valley; but after the rout at Gujerat, he was driven out by a British force, and narrowly escaped with his life into his own territory. Henceforth he submitted to the loss of Peshawar. In 1853-55 he concluded treaties of friendship with Sir John Lawrence, the Chief Commissioner of the Punjab. In 1856-57 Persia again besieged Herat. The British helped the Dost with money and arms, and sent a British expedition to the Persian Gulf, until the Shah withdrew from Herat. Henceforth the British government found a faithful ally in Dost Mohammed Khan. During the sepoy mutinies of 1857, which will be described in the next chapter, when British power was paralysed for a moment in Northern India, the old Dost remained loyal throughout to British supremacy. He died at Herat in 1863.

22. **Summary.** — British advance into Central Asia has five stages. First, the Afghan wars of 1838–42, which ended in the withdrawal of British influence to the eastern bank of the Sutlej. Second, the conquest of Sind, followed by the war in Gwalior, which restored British prestige in all the frontier States. Third, the Sikh invasion of 1845–46, which ended in the establishment of a double government in the Punjab under a nominal Maharaja, like that which Lord Clive introduced in Bengal and Behar under a nominal Padishah. Fourth, the Sikh revolt in 1848–49, which ended in the conquest of the Punjab, the introduction of British rule, and the triumph of order and law. Fifth, the awakening of Dost Mohammed Khan, Amir of Afghanistan, to a sense of his position and interest in Central Asia, and his final acceptance of the British alliance.

CHAPTER XII.

LORD DALHOUSIE, 1848-56: LORD CANNING: SEPOY MUTINIES, 1857-58.

1. British Rule in the Punjab.—2. Non-Regulation.—3. Public Works: Canals, Roads, Bridges, Railways, and Telegraphs.—4. Conquests and Annexations: Pegu, Nagpore, Oudh.—5. India Bill of 1853: new Civil Service and Legislative Council.—6. Moghul "King" at Delhi.—7. LORD CANNING, 1856: British Rule in Oudh, 1856–57.—8. Sepoy Armies: Madras, Bombay, and Bengal.—9. Disaffection of the Bengal Army: Greased Cartridges, 1857.—10. Mutiny at Meerut, near Delhi, May, 1857.—11. Revolt at Delhi: Proclamation of the Padishah.—12. Siege of Delhi, May to September, 1857.—13. Insurrection in the North-West Provinces and Oudh.—14. Agra and Lucknow.—15. British Advance from Calcutta.—16. Sepoy Mutiny at Cawnpore, June, 1857.—17. Treachery of Nana Sahib.—18. Massacres: Flight of Nana Sahib.—19. End of the Sepoy Mutinies, 1857–8.—20. India under the Crown, 1858.—21. Summary.

1. British Rule in the Punjab.—The Punjab was governed for a while by a Board of three. Sir Henry Lawrence was president, Sir John Lawrence was revenue member, and Sir Robert Montgomery was judicial member. But the Board did not answer. Sir John Lawrence had been appointed Commissioner of Jullunder by Lord Hardinge, and he was now appointed Chief Commissioner of the Punjab by Lord Dalhousie. Sir Robert Montgomery was Judicial Commissioner and controlled the law courts. There was no Governor in Council; no Sudder or Supreme

Court. Sir John Lawrence was Governor, and Sir Robert Montgomery was Chief Judge.

2. **Non-Regulation.**—The Punjab was parcelled into divisions, each under a commissioner; and into districts, each under a deputy commissioner. The commissioner of a division controlled the deputy commissioners of three, four, or more districts. The patriarchal idea ran through the whole system. The deputy commissioner of a district was collector, magistrate, and judge in his district. Below him were assistants and subordinates, European and Asiatic. The "regulations" of the old Presidencies were modified in the Punjab by local usages, tribal customs, and the different religious institutions of Sikhs, Mohammedans, and Hindus. The revenue Survey and Settlement followed that of the North-West Provinces, but was adapted to local circumstances. All the local officials were entrusted with large discretionary powers, and the Punjab was known as a "non-regulation" province.

3. **Public Works: Canals, Roads, Bridges, Railways, and Telegraphs.**—The Punjab was Lord Dalhousie's pride and glory. He opened it out with roads and bridges, and made it a model province. In like manner he laboured to make British India a model empire according to western ideas of civilization. He pushed on the great Ganges canal and its branches, which water the North West Provinces for 3,000 miles and are navigable for 600. The work had been begun some thirty years before. It was planned and completed by Sir Proby Cautley, and opened by Lord Dalhousie. In like manner the grand trunk road between Bengal and the north-west frontier was bridged and metalled, and brought to a conclusion. For the first time in recorded history mail carts and carriages ran from Calcutta to Delhi, Lahore and

Peshawar. Lord Dalhousie planned the systems of railways and telegraphs which linked every Presidency and province in India. He gave India a postage of half an anna, or three farthings a letter; lit up Calcutta with gas; and opened out the Sunderbunds to the sea breezes. These malarious jungles had poisoned every wind that blew from the south since the foundation of Calcutta. In the present day the winds from the south are fresh from the Bay of Bengal, and bring life and health instead of fever.

4. **Conquests and Annexations: Pegu, Nagpore, Oudh.**—In 1852 Lord Dalhousie resented the outrages of Burmese officials on British subjects, and insults to the British flag, by sending an expedition up the river Irrawaddy and conquering Pegu. He annexed the principality of Nagpore on the death of the Raja whom Lord Hastings had placed upon the throne as an infant, and who had neglected his people and abandoned himself to vicious indulgences. He annexed Oudh territory by deposing an effete dynasty, which had been deaf to the warnings and remonstrances of half a century, and presumed on British forbearance until its misrule and oppression had become intolerable. Since his time annexation has ceased to be a policy. In cases of cruelty and misrule, the British government prefers to depose a prince and accept a successor, rather than to confiscate a principality and extinguish a dynasty.

5. **India Bill of 1853: New Civil Service and Legislative Council.**—In 1853, when the charter of 1833 had expired, Parliament hesitated to abolish the East India Company, but would not renew the charter. It deprived the directors of the privilege of nominating members of the Indian Civil Service, and ordered that all candidates should be selected by competitive examination. It enlarged the Legislative

Council of Bengal into a Legislative Council for all India. Every Presidency was to send a civil servant to Calcutta to sit in the Council as a representative member. The Chief Justice and one puisne judge in the Supreme Court at Calcutta were also appointed members. The sittings of the new Legislative Council began in 1854 with the revision of the Penal Code for all British India, which had been drafted by Lord Macaulay.

6. **Moghul "King" at Delhi.**—After the Mahratta war of 1803–5, Shah Alam, the nominal "king" or Padishah at Delhi, was taken under British protection. He had long been a puppet in the hands of the Mahrattas, who collected chout and revenue in his name. The British respected him as a relic of an extinct dynasty, which had been maintained by pensionary support for political reasons that had long ceased to exist. Shah Alam was succeeded by a line of princes whose children and grandchildren multiplied exceedingly; and Lord Dalhousie arranged that when the reigning "king" was gathered to his fathers, his successor would remove the whole family to the Kutub, an old royal residence some miles from Delhi.

7. **Lord Canning, 1856–62: British Rule in Oudh, 1856–57.**—Lord Dalhousie left India in 1856, and was succeeded by Lord Canning. By this time Oudh had been brought under British administration as a non-regulation province. The talukdars disliked the change. During the anarchy of the previous generation, many had acquired possession of large areas of villages, and ignored or stamped out the rights of village proprietors, joint or otherwise. But the British authorities began a new Survey and Settlement, on the same system as in the North-West Provinces. Village rights had been respected,

whilst those of talukdars had been ignored or referred for consideration to the law courts. The people of Lucknow, especially the classes who battened on the luxury and vices of the dethroned prince and his courtiers, were equally impoverished and disaffected. At last Sir Henry Lawrence was appointed Chief Commissioner, and was expected to redress grievances and remove discontent.

8. **Sepoy Armies: Madras, Bombay, and Bengal.**—Each of the three older Presidencies had its own sepoy army, commanded by British officers. The Madras army of the south and the Bombay army of the Deccan were under their respective governments. The Bengal army garrisoned the whole of northern India, including Bengal, the North-West Provinces, Oudh, and the Punjab. Indeed the term "Bengal army" was a misnomer, for it was not recruited in Bengal proper, but from the military races of Hindustan. For more than half a century Oudh had been the chief recruiting ground.

9. **Disaffection of the Bengal Army: Greased Cartridges, 1857.**—In Madras and Bombay the sepoys were as loyal as ever, but there was disaffection in the Bengal army. Cartridges in those days were made of paper. In loading the musket, the sepoy or soldier bit off the end of the cartridge with his teeth, and poured the powder into the barrel, before ramming down the bullet. A new cartridge was introduced for Enfield rifles. It was waxed or greased. Evil speakers insinuated that the grease was taken from the fat of cows and swine; that the British government was bent on destroying caste by making Hindu sepoys taste beef, and destroying Islam by making Mohammedan sepoys taste pork. The mutiny began at Barrackpore, sixteen miles from Calcutta, and at Berhampore.

about one hundred miles to the northward. The sepoys refused to accept the cartridges, and rose against their European officers. The outbreak was suppressed at both cantonments, and two sepoy regiments were disbanded. Next followed an outbreak at Lucknow, but that was promptly put down by Sir Henry Lawrence. Meanwhile the obnoxious cartridges were withdrawn, and it was hoped that the scare was dying out.

10. **Mutiny at Meerut, near Delhi, May, 1857.**—Suddenly the disaffection broke out at Meerut, forty miles from Delhi, and 1,000 miles from Calcutta. The cantonment at Meerut covered an area of five miles, and was the largest in India. The European soldiers lived in barracks at one end; the sepoys lived at the other end in lines of huts in the Indian fashion. Many sepoys refused to receive any cartridges whatever, not even the old pattern which their forefathers had used for generations. Court-martials were held, and something like a hundred mutineers were sent to jail. One hot Sunday in May, when the Europeans were at church, or resting through the heat, the sepoys were getting excited in their huts, and brooding over their wrongs. Suddenly at evening time they seized their arms, rushed out of their lines, shot down every European they met, not excepting ladies and children, broke into houses and bungalows, and set them on fire, released 1,500 prisoners from the jail, and then marched off to Delhi, before the Europeans at the barracks, who had heard of the outbreak, could reach the lines.

11. **Revolt at Delhi: Proclamation of the Padishah.**—There were three sepoy regiments at Delhi, cantoned on the Ridge outside the city. Round about them were the bungalows of the British officers in command, but there was no European regiment at Delhi. The mutineer cavalry from Meerut arrived on

Monday morning, and were joined by the Delhi sepoys. They proclaimed the old Moghul "king" to be Emperor of Hindustan. They butchered an English chaplain, and fifty women and children who had taken refuge in the palace. The British officers on the Ridge escaped as they best could with their wives and children.

12. **Siege of Delhi, May to September, 1857.**—For nearly five months, from May to September, 1857, the city of Delhi was at the mercy of the rebels. European and Ghorka regiments were marched down from the stations on the Himalayas and re-occupied the Ridge. Sikh regiments were sent from the Punjab, together with batteries of artillery, by Sir John Lawrence, the chief commissioner. But Delhi was strongly fortified, and could not be captured without a siege train, and it was not until the 20th of September that the city was taken by storm.

13. **Insurrection in the North-West Provinces and Oudh.**—Meanwhile the Bengal sepoys, as they were called, broke out in mutiny at every military station in Northern India. They shot their European officers, set fire to the bungalows, and plundered the treasuries. Many marched off to Delhi and joined the rebels. Others tried to escape with their booty to their several homes; and unknown numbers were robbed and murdered on the way. Indeed all the brigands and bad characters in Northern India appeared to have broken loose, and sacked and slaughtered without regard to race or creed.

14. **Agra and Lucknow.**—In the North-West Provinces certain landholders who had been discontented with the Survey and Settlement, made common cause with the rebels. In Oudh the talukdars joined the rebels with their retainers. Even the

village proprietors, who had recovered their rights to the land under the recent Survey and Settlement, were so panic-stricken by the anarchy that they sought refuge under the walls of the fortresses of their talukdars who had previously treated them as tenants without any rights at all. The result was that the Europeans were shut up in the fortress at Agra, the capital of the North-West Provinces, and in the British Residency at Lucknow, the capital of Oudh, waiting for the advance of a relieving army from Bengal.

15. **British Advance from Calcutta.**—Lord Canning at Calcutta was collecting British forces from all quarters to clear the way to the north-west. In June Colonel Neill, with a small body of Europeans, pushed on to Patna, Benares and Allahabad. In July General Havelock arrived at Allahabad with reinforcements of Europeans, and prepared to advance by way of Cawnpore on the Ganges to the relief of Lucknow.

16. **Sepoy Mutiny at Cawnpore, June, 1857.**—Meanwhile there had been terrible scenes at Cawnpore. Four sepoy regiments had broken out in mutiny. They had not attacked their British officers, but had set out to join the rebels at Delhi. General Sir Hugh Wheeler, who commanded the station, had no Europeans available but the regimental officers. He had a large number of ladies on his hands whose husbands were at Lucknow. He had retired with the whole party to some deserted barracks, and prepared to hold the rebels at bay. The sepoys would have gone on to Delhi, but a Mahratta Brahman, named Nana Sahib, persuaded them to return by declaring that vast treasures were hidden in the barracks.

17. **Treachery of Nana Sahib.**—Nana Sahib was an adopted son of Baji Rao, the last of the

Peishwas, who had lost his throne and kingdom in 1817-18. Baji Rao had lived on a pension near Cawnpore until his death in 1853. (Chap. ix. § 23.) Lord Dalhousie permitted Nana Sahib to inherit the wealth of the ex-Peishwa, but not his pension, which had lapsed to the British government. This was the grievance of the Nana. Accordingly he professed the utmost loyalty and friendship for the British until the sepoys broke out in mutiny, and then he incited the rebels to make repeated assaults on the beleaguered Europeans.

18. **Massacres: Flight of Nana Sahib.**—But Nana Sahib could not storm the barracks. The Europeans were resolved to resist unto death, and would have cut their way through the rebels or died sword in hand, but they would not abandon the women and children. At last Nana Sahib solemnly swore that he would send all the besieged in safety to Allahabad if they would only surrender their arms. The terms were accepted. Forty boats were prepared to carry the besieged down the Ganges. The whole party embarked, and then Nana Sahib ordered the rebels to fire on the boats and compel the victims to disembark. The Europeans were landed and the men were bound and shot. The women and children were shut up in a large building. Meanwhile General Havelock was advancing towards Cawnpore. The rebels went to meet him but were utterly routed. The infamous Nana Sahib, maddened by defeat, ordered all the women and children to be butchered and thrown into a well. Henceforth he was a fugitive. Little more was heard of him, and it is generally believed that he perished miserably in the jungle.

19. **End of the Sepoy Mutinies, 1857-8.**—The British Residency at Lucknow was relieved by General Havelock and Sir James Outram in

September, 1857. Sir Henry Lawrence had been killed by the bursting of a shell. Delhi had fallen, Agra was relieved, and the sepoy mutinies were virtually over. The North-West Provinces were cleared of rebels, and communications were opened from Bengal to the Punjab. British reinforcements in overwhelming numbers reached India round the Cape. Oudh was reconquered by Sir Colin Campell, afterwards Lord Clyde. Central India was restored to order by Sir Hugh Rose, afterwards Lord Strathnairn.

20. **India under the Crown, 1858.**—In 1858 the East India Company was abolished by Parliament, and the direct government of India by the Crown was announced by Royal Proclamation. The Court of Directors and Board of Control were superseded by a Secretary of State for India in Council. The Governor-General became Viceroy of India.

21. **Summary.**—The administrations of Lords Dalhousie and Canning are the beginnings of the modern history of India. Whatever feelings may have been excited by the innovations and annexations of Lord Dalhousie, they have long since died out, like the cries of "no gas" and "no railroad," which were not unfrequently raised by our fathers. Anarchy and misrule have vanished for ever from the Punjab and Oudh. Lord Canning fell on evil times. The sepoy mutinies are the saddest episode in Indian history, but a recurrence is next to impossible. The sepoys will never again be induced to believe that the British government planned to destroy their religion and caste by the use of greased cartridges; whilst all quarters of the Empire are linked together, not only by electricity and steam, but by a common loyalty to the British Crown.

CHAPTER XIII.

BRITISH CROWN: QUEEN AND EMPRESS, 1858–90.

1. Royal Proclamation.—2. LORD CANNING, 1858–62: Constitutional Changes.—3. Expansion of British India: Three Presidencies—Bengal, Madras, and Bombay.—4. Governor-General of Bengal: Warren Hastings to Lord William Bentinck, 1774–1834.—5. Governor-General of India, 1834: Legislative Councils of 1834, 1854, 1862.—6. Lieutenant-Governors: North-West Provinces, Bengal and Punjab.—7. Chief Commissioners: Oudh, Central Provinces, British Burma.—8. Foreign or Political Affairs: Indian Cabinet.—9. LORD ELGIN, 1862–63: Death of Dost Mohammed Khan, 1863.—10. War against the Wahabis of Sitana.—11. LORD LAWRENCE, 1864–69: War against Bhutan.—12. LORD MAYO, 1869–72: Afghanistan Affairs.—13. LORD NORTHBROOK, 1872–76.—14. LORD LYTTON, 1876–80: Proclamation of the Empress of India.—15. Famine of 1877.—16. Second War in Afghanistan, 1878–79.—17. Massacre of Sir Louis Cavagnari and Escort at Kabul.—18. LORD RIPON, 1880–84: Abdur Rahman Khan, Amir.—19. LORD DUFFERIN, 1884–88: Conquest of Upper Burma or Ava.—20. LORD LANSDOWNE, 1888–90.—21. Summary.

1. **Royal Proclamation.**—The Royal Proclamation of 1858 might be likened to the rainbow in the cloud after the deluge. It was a new covenant with India. It confirmed all existing rights, repudiated all thought of interfering with caste or religion, and asserted the sovereignty of Her Majesty the Queen. The East India Company passed away, and the British Crown was supreme.

2. **Lord Canning, 1858-62: Constitutional Changes.**—Lord Canning was Viceroy of India for three years after the mutinies. Meanwhile the Com-

pany's army was amalgamated with the Royal army. Local European troops were transferred to the Queen's service, and sepoy battalions were re-organized and officered on the irregular system. The Sudder and Supreme Courts at Calcutta, Madras and Bombay, were amalgamated into High Courts, and an Asiatic Judge in each Court sat for the first time on the same bench as the British Judges. The Legislative Council for all India was enlarged by the addition of non-official members, European and Asiatic, nominated by the Executive. A local Legislative Council was created at Calcutta, Madras and Bombay, for making laws under the sanction of the Government of India for their respective Presidencies. It comprised the old Executive Council, with the addition of non-official members, European and Asiatic, nominated by the local Government.

3. Expansion of British India: Three Presidencies—Bengal, Madras and Bombay.—The expansion of the British empire in India was originally that of factories into provinces. Calcutta, Madras and Bombay were originally factories, more or less fortified, and dotted round with the houses and gardens of British settlers. At Calcutta and Madras the natives lived in a distinct quarter which was known as "black town." At Bombay there was less exclusiveness. Each of the three settlements was called a Presidency, because each was governed by a President and Council. After the battle of Plassy territories were added to the Presidencies. Bengal fell into the hands of the British at Calcutta by a revolution which seemed a miracle. Madras obtained grants of villages and districts in return for services rendered to Nawabs of the Carnatic. Bombay, however, was isolated by Mahrattas, and acquired no additional territories from the days of Charles II. to those of George III.

4. Governor-General of Bengal: Warren Hastings to Lord William Bentinck, 1774-1834. — When Warren Hastings was Governor-General of Bengal in 1774, he ruled a territory larger than Great Britain and Ireland. At the same time Madras was less than Wales, and Bombay was smaller than the Isle of Wight. Sixty years later, the Bengal Presidency extended westward to the river Sutlej. It was divided into Lower and Upper Provinces, but the Governor-General of Bengal still ruled the whole as included in the Bengal Presidency, whilst controlling the political and foreign relations of Madras and Bombay as in the days of Warren Hastings.

5. Governor-General of India, 1834: Legislative Councils of 1834, 1854, 1862.—In 1834 Lord William Bentinck was created Governor-General of India under the Charter Act of 1833. Under the same Act the Governor-General of India and his Bengal Council were invested with the control of the finances of all three Presidencies. Above all the Governor-General of India and his Bengal Council were converted into a Legislative Council for all India, with exclusive power to make laws for Madras and Bombay as well as for Bengal. Yet at this time Madras was larger than Great Britain and Ireland; Bombay, which had not as yet acquired Sind, was larger than England and Wales; and the people of the three Presidencies were as different from each other in race and language as the people of European nations. This exclusive system was reformed in 1854 by the addition of representative civil servants from the other Presidencies, and still more so in 1862 by the addition of non-official members.

6. Lieutenant-Governors: North-West Provinces, Bengal, and Punjab.—In 1834 Lord

William Bentinck was relieved from some of the work by the formation of the North-West Provinces into a separate administration under a Lieutenant-Governor. In 1854 Lord Dalhousie was relieved by the separation of Bengal under a similar authority. In 1859 Lord Canning was relieved by the conversion of the Punjab into a Lieutenant-Governorship under Sir John Lawrence. These Lieutenant-Governors were not British statesmen appointed by the Crown as in the three Presidencies, but Indian civil servants appointed by the Governor-General.

7. **Chief Commissioners: Oudh, Central Provinces, British Burma.**—Oudh had been placed under a Chief Commissioner in 1856. In 1861 Lord Canning placed the Central Provinces, including the territory of Nagpore, under a Chief Commissioner. At the same time British Burma, including Arakan, Tenasserim, and Pegu, was placed under a similar administration.

8. **Foreign or Political Affairs: Indian Cabinet.**—The Foreign Office at Calcutta was created by Warren Hastings after Philip Francis returned to England. Henceforth Warren Hastings kept the conduct of Foreign and Political affairs in his own hands. The Foreign included European powers who had relations with India. The Political included Asiatic States owing allegiance to British supremacy. Every Governor-General since the days of Warren Hastings has been his own Foreign and Political Minister. He is President in a Council of six members, corresponding to six departments, namely, Foreign, Home, Financial, Revenue, Military, and Legislative. Every member of Council is thus a Cabinet Minister, with a Secretary to carry on the business of his department; the whole forming the Government of India as distinct from the Legislative Council which makes the laws.

9. Lord Elgin, 1862–63: Death of Dost Mohammed Khan, 1863.—Lord Canning left India in 1862, but died in England the same year, and was buried in Westminster Abbey. Lord Elgin succeeded in 1862. Dost Mohammed Khan died in 1863 as already seen. He was succeeded by a younger son, Shere Ali Khan, to the exclusion of the first-born, Afzul Khan. Within a few months the dissatisfaction at this exclusion led to a general war between the brothers.

10. War against the Wahabis of Sitana.—Lord Elgin sent an expedition against the Wahabi fanatics at Sitana beyond the north-west frontier. They had been guilty of robbery and murder within our border, and carried off British subjects as prisoners for ransom; and they were recruited in men and money from fanatics of the same religion who resided in Bengal. Lord Elgin died at Dharmsala on the Himálaya shortly after the beginning of hostilities.

11. Lord Lawrence, 1864–69: War against Bhutan.—Sir John, afterwards Lord Lawrence, succeeded in 1864. The Sitana expedition was brought to a close, and the fanatics driven from their strongholds. Another war was declared against Bhutan in the Himálaya, to the eastward of Nipal. The Bhutanese had harried villages in Bengal proper, and taken away the villagers as slaves. A British envoy was sent to demand redress, but was insulted by the Bhutanese authorities. War was declared. A border territory known as the Dooars was confiscated; and the Bhutan government was bound over to prevent all such raids for the future. Lord Lawrence completed the land settlement in Oudh, and the rights of talukdars and ryots were ascertained and recorded. His term of office was marked by a fearful famine in Orissa, and another in Bundelkund and western Hindustan. Local officers were called upon to take every possible means to avert starvation. Lord Lawrence left India in 1869. He died in 1879, and was buried in Westminster Abbey.

12. **Lord Mayo, 1869–72: Afghanistan Affairs.**—In 1868 the fratricidal war in Afghanistan was over. Afzul Khan was dead, and his son Abdur Rahman Khan was a political refugee. Shere Ali Khan had gained the throne and was recognized as Amir. Lord Mayo held a conference with Shere Ali Khan at Umballa, and won his confidence but would not interfere in his domestic wars. Lord Mayo entertained His Royal Highness the Duke of Edinburgh; the first of a series of royal visits to India. He devoted much time and energy to public works and financial reforms, and his administration promised to be most successful. In 1872 he paid a visit to Rangoon, and then to the convict settlement in the Andaman Islands. At Port Blair he was stabbed to death by an Afghan murderer who had been condemned to imprisonment for life, and an active career was brought suddenly to a close.

13. **Lord Northbrook, 1872–76.**—Lord Northbrook averted a terrible famine in Bengal by State relief. He dethroned the Gaekwar of Baroda for gross misrule, and for an attempt to poison the British Resident. He refrained from annexing his territories, and accepted an adopted heir as the future ruler of Baroda. During his administration India was visited by His Royal Highness the Prince of Wales, who was received on all sides with enthusiastic loyalty.

14. **Lord Lytton, 1876–80: Proclamation of the Empress of India.**—On the 1st January,

1877, Her Majesty Queen Victoria was proclaimed Empress of India at an Imperial Assemblage at Delhi, the most striking and magnificent gathering in the history of the British empire in Asia. For the first time in the history of India the chiefs and princes of India forgot their feuds and met as friends under the canopy of British sovereignty.

15. **Famine of 1877.**—Shortly afterwards Southern India was desolated by a famine which extended northwards into Hindustan, and was more widely spread than any previous drought. Starving masses of Hindus and Mohammedans were fed at a cost of eleven millions sterling. The extension of railways will mitigate such terrible visitations for the future.

16. **Second War in Afghanistan, 1878–79.**—Later on Lord Lytton was drawn into a war with Afghanistan. Shere Ali Khan had been trimming between Great Britain and Russia. At last he received a Russian envoy at Kabul, and refused to admit a friendly mission from Lord Lytton. British armies entered Afghanistan by three passes—the Khyber, the Kurram and the Bolan. Shere Ali fled away and died. His eldest son Yakub Khan was recognized by Lord Lytton as Amir of Afghanistan.

17. **Massacre of Sir Louis Cavagnari and Escort at Kabul.**—Yakub Khan agreed to receive a British Resident at Kabul. He welcomed the coming of Sir Louis Cavagnari, and provided quarters. Suddenly the Resident and his escort were environed by the army of Yakub Khan, overpowered and slaughtered. Yakub Khan abdicated the throne and was deported to British India.

18. **Lord Ripon, 1880–84: Abdur Rahman Khan, Amir.**—The new Viceroy brought the war

in Afghanistan to a close. Abdur Rahman claimed the throne as the eldest son of Afzul Khan, the first-born of Dost Mohammed. On the other hand Ayub Khan, the younger brother of Yakub, was bent on seizing the throne by force of arms. He attacked a British force at Maimand, about thirty miles from Kandahar, and gained a momentary advantage. General Frederic Roberts however marched his forces 325 miles from Kabul to Kandahar within twenty-one days, and utterly routed Ayub Khan. Abdur Rahman was recognized by Lord Ripon as Amir of Afghanistan, and Ayub Khan fled into Persia.

19. **Lord Dufferin, 1884–88: Conquest of Upper Burmah or Ava.**—Lord Dufferin confirmed the peace with Afghanistan, and settled a vexed frontier question which had been raised by Russia. He put an end to the cruelties, oppressions, and vacillations of the Burmese ruler by the conquest of the territory and extinction of the dynasty. Lady Dufferin cultivated the society of Indian ladies, and introduced female medical attendants. Her Majesty the Empress warmly sympathised with her efforts, which promoted the happiness of Indian wives and mothers, and the well-being of their children. During the administration of Lord Dufferin the Jubilee of Her Majesty the Empress was celebrated in 1887 with the utmost enthusiasm by all classes and races in India; and His Royal Highness the Duke of Connaught served as Commander-in-Chief of the Bombay army.

20. **Lord Lansdowne, 1888–1890.**—The brief history is here brought to a close. Hitherto Lord Lansdowne has been engaged in deciding several questions connected with the public service, the future of State education, and the further development of the Anglo-Indian constitution. His administration has

been marked by the visit of His Royal Highness Prince Albert Victor, the eldest son of the Prince of Wales.

21. **Summary.**—Since the Sepoy mutinies of 1857–58, peace has been restored to India and British supremacy re-established. Legislative Councils have been re-constituted and enlarged, and the Sudder and Supreme Courts have been amalgamated into High Courts. Within the last few years a Legislative Council has been given to the Lieutenant-Governor of the North-West Provinces; and a High Court has been created at Allahabad. In the Punjab a Chief Court has been created at Lahore. The second war in Afghanistan and the conquest of Upper Burmah have extended British influence further and further towards Persia on one side and China on the other. India has been brought nearer to Europe by the Suez Canal, and a succession of Royal visits have confirmed her people in their loyalty to the British Crown. These events make up the current history. Movements, however, are at work beneath the surface, which are carrying India into an unknown future. The vast development of State education, the extension of railways and telegraphs, the decay of personal government, and the establishment of the reign of law, will stamp the era for all time. Non-regulation is passing away for ever.